Gospel-Centered Spirituality

To Amy —

With gratitude for your wonderful
assistance with the placement of an intern
at Mary & Martha. Connie & I are so
pleased and blessed by your helpfulness.

May what is shared herein bless
you on your journey.

Allan H. Sager

Gospel-Centered Spirituality

An Introduction to
Our Spiritual Journey

Allan H. Sager

Augsburg ∾ Minneapolis

GOSPEL-CENTERED SPIRITUALITY
An Introduction to Our Spiritual Journey

Cover design: Lecy Design

Library of Congress Cataloging-in-Publication Data
Sager, Allan H., 1934–
    Gospel-centered spirituality: an introduction to our spiritual
journey / Allan H. Sager.
        p. cm.
    Includes bibliographical references.
    ISBN 0-8066-2440-X
    1. Spiritual life—Lutheran authors. 2. Grace (Theology)
I. Title.
BV 4501.2.S155   1990   89-71081
248—dc20   CIP

The paper used in this publication meets the minimum requirements of American National Standard for Information Sciences—Permanence of Paper for Printed Library Materials, ANSI Z329.48-1984.

Manufactured in the U.S.A.   9-2440

94   93   2   3   4   5   6   7   8   9   10

To Erline, my wife,
whose graciousness enhances her beauty
as my companion on the journey of faith

To daughter Denise,
who teaches well
the venturesomeness of faith

To daughter Monica,
whose vivaciousness illustrates
the vitality and contagion of faith

Contents

Preface

In recent years there has been increasing interest among Christians in the subject of spirituality. In my work as a seminary professor for contextual education, I have been asked to make a number of presentations on various topics in spirituality to lay persons, clergy, and church officials. I have therefore been challenged to become better informed so that I might offer some guidance to others. Along the way I have discovered something of the immensity of the subject of spirituality and that among Christians there exists a great deal of confusion as to what spirituality really is.

This book approaches spirituality from a gospel-centered viewpoint. The gospel is the central treasure of the church, the content of its preaching and teaching, the heartbeat of its witness through mission and service. Spirituality that is gospel-centered is a spirituality that is anchored in the *evangel* or good news of God's grace in Jesus Christ. The purpose of this book is twofold: to offer a gospel-centered perspective on the nature of Christian spirituality and to introduce a variety of topics in spirituality to those unacquainted with the Christian spiritual tradition.

As an evangelical (gospel-oriented) Christian, I believe that spirituality must be understood in the context of God's grace. True spirituality moves, I am persuaded, with the power and pace of grace. It recognizes that pride can lurk behind any spiritual activity, no matter how noble it may appear. But it also knows that where

Christ is active in the life of a believer, the most ordinary of human activities can be an expression of spirituality. While a gospel-centered spirituality says *no* to any suggestion that human activity can add something to God's grace, it says *yes* to those pursuits that focus on Christ and therefore encourage a richer and deeper experience of that grace.

Grace is central and primary. Spirituality is anchored in, flows out of, returns to, and blossoms from life in grace. What we have too much of in the church are worn-out directions aimed at willful self-actualization, as if we could—if we only would—start behaving like Christians should behave. The admonitions to alter our moral course are pious enough and the appeals to abdicate our egocentric thrones are noble enough. But too seldom are they linked with that evangelical word of empowerment through the gospel that declares the reality of our new life in Christ and invites us to experience that life to the fullest.

As an evangelical Lutheran, I have no intent to fashion a new bondage of the spirit. But I firmly believe that there are practices that help a person attend to the presence of Christ and that therefore may properly be called spiritual. Topics frequently included under the category of spirituality are numerous, and in many cases the amount of literature available is vast. If I were here to discuss each topic in depth, this book would become unmanageably long. Instead, in Part Two, I have simply introduced a number of topics and then provided an annotated bibliography for each one. While by no means exhaustive, the bibliographies do provide suggestions for further reading.

Being a Christian is not a solitary affair. Yet much that is said and written about spirituality is expressed in highly individualistic terms and can be construed as concerned with helping *individuals* build intimacy in their personal relationship with God. I urge readers to remain focused on the large, communal context of *our* faith, *our* hope, and *our* love. The Lord's Prayer serves as a prime model in this regard. One may pray it personally and individually, to be sure, but the "Our Father," "our daily bread," and "our sins" recital reminds us of our eternal placement in the community of faith.

I speak now especially to those who come to this book with the query: How can I best develop my spiritual life so I can come to share it with others? That sounds laudable, but allowing the question to remain cast in that manner tends to perpetuate the separation of spiritual nurture from life in community. A better query would be: Where do we find the community of faith to which the Spirit of God descends, in which the Word and sacraments are powerfully alive, and from which God's message of hope and love can be brought as a light and leaven into the world?

We are in community because we have received the same divine breath, have been given a heart set aflame by the same divine fire, and have been embraced by the same divine love. That's both a consoling and confronting realization. It is consoling to realize that the living God actively works to bond us in a unity we most long for, and confronting to realize that we are impotent to heal our own brokenness. From beginning to end, spirituality is gospel-centered.

Allan H. Sager

Acknowledgments

Many have assisted to make this book possible. Seminary class-mate, William Behrends, then with the Office of Support to Ministries of The American Lutheran Church, first invited a study document on spirituality along with his invitation that my wife and I participate in a series of Spirituality and Stress Workshops for Lutheran bishops and their staffs. Following that experience in 1984–85, he nudged extension of that work by sharing it with Roland Seboldt, then director of book development for Augsburg Publishing House, who provided supportive encouragement and instruction.

The shaping of this book owes most to Robert Moluf, editorial director of Augsburg books. He mixed incisive editing expertise with informed theological judgment to shepherd this work to completion.

The Board of Directors of Trinity Lutheran Seminary granted a sabbatical which assured the needed reading/reflecting/writing time. Dr. James C. Childs Jr., Academic Dean, was instrumental in assembling funds for travel, resource acquisitions, and other research expenses.

My wife, Erline, provided that balance of supportive presence, balanced critique, and safeguarding of solitude which helped to insure the meeting of publication deadlines.

Much of this material has been presented in a variety of lecture modes. Both appreciative and critical comments by the auditors have influenced the content of this book. To all of these, the named and unnamed, I share an acknowledgment of thanks.

Part One | A Foundation for Christian Spirituality

1 | Discovering the Center

A t birth we are born into a life on earth. At baptism we are born into a life in the dominion of God. In neither birth do we take the initiative. Both are gifts from God.

I fully understand neither. Both are full of mystery and miracle.

For me, it was the fourth Sunday in September, 1934. I was too young to know what was happening that Sunday as water was placed on my head while some precious promises were declared, Scripture was read, and my parents and sponsors made some commitments about providing Christian training for that little son of Gus and Estella Sager.

I was baptized. God was claiming me. Before I even had the gift of speech to request adoption into that family of God, God reached out to embrace me. God's undeserved love flooded into my life. I became a Christian. I was given a name and a birthright. I was given identity as a child of God and assigned worth in the realm of God. I became an heir to heaven.

Baptism has always been for me one of the clearest, most dramatic demonstrations of our grace-filled God. It is one of the best possible grace sermons enacted sacramentally. God reaches out to a totally helpless infant—dependent in every way: needing to be fed, burped, clothed, and changed. The infant is totally unaware of the miracle

taking place at that time. Oh, perhaps the infant is discomforted
a bit by water on the head, but still totally oblivious to the meaning
of it all. It's not as though the babe doesn't need the forgiving and
transforming love of God. If you don't think there is as much
preoccupation with self in an infant as there is in anybody else,
then you haven't spent much time with children!

To insist that a person have conscious awareness of God's graciousness and let it be a liberating and redeeming power for one's
life—all as a condition for baptism—is to give too much credit to
our freedom and too little to our bondage in sin. In baptism, God
is the divine actor. We are the recipients of God's unmotivated-by-
us and even unsolicited-by-us favor. What a powerful event! What
a miracle of grace! What a stirring reminder to me even now that
God's grace has acted on my behalf even when I'm not thinking of
God or making conscious effort to be close to God.

Baptism—a birthing by grace for which I took no personal initiative.

Spirituality after Dark

Late one night Jesus and Nicodemus, a ruler of the Jews, had
quite a conversation about this special birthing process (see John
3).

Jesus told Nicodemus: "Unless one is born anew, . . . unless one
is born of water and the Spirit, one cannot enter the dominion of
God. That which is born of the flesh is flesh, and that which is
born of the Spirit is spirit" (John 3:3, 5-6).

Nicodemus was all confused about this birthing talk and was
caught up in a hopeless literalism. "How can a person be born when
that person is old? Can one enter a second time into the womb
and be born?" (John 3:4). Jesus was talking about a spiritual rebirth,
the type of which Titus 3:5 speaks when it calls baptism "the washing
of regeneration." That refers to a new beginning, a spiritual cleansing, a washing that affords new life. Nicodemus, though a member
of the Sanhedrin, the official Jewish court, had trouble understanding this brand of spirituality.

"What? The kingdom of God is entered, not by moral achievement, but by a transformation wrought by God?" Nicodemus might

have said. "Why, I'm a Pharisee, the most devout among the Jews. Do you mean to tell me, Jesus, that my devout devotions and devoted devoutness aren't the basis for kingdom membership?"

Counting with the CEO of the Universe

Much of my counseling ministry through the years has dealt with problems that, at root, have to do with a poor self-image. I have seen so many people try to find some kind of personal validation that can firm up their sagging self-esteem.

Seeking validation from others.   Many people today are seeking some measure of affirmation from meaningful relationships with others. They seek such "horizontal" validation from a spouse, child, significant other, neighbor, friend, or work colleague. Tremendous energies and untold amounts of time are poured into the cultivation of these relationships.

Such affirmation by others provides many of the nutrients needed for a healthy self-image. But we run into difficulties when our basic self-image becomes overly dependent on what people think of us. Validation of ourselves by others is good but ultimately inadequate. Regardless of the importance, goodness, or beauty of our relationships, they cannot provide us with complete fulfillment. If we become too dependent on them, they can tyrannize us. We can be freed from such tyranny only when we come to see that our basic sense of self-worth must come from a different source.

Seeking validation from within.   Some people try to protect themselves from the vagaries of others' opinions by seeking a sense of validation from themselves. They try to establish a self-image so secure that it needs no outside affirmation or support. This tactic is as old as the folk wisdom that declares that all the water in the ocean cannot sink a ship unless it gets inside.

Psychologists are quick to tell us that certain exercises can be helpful in establishing a positive self-image for ourselves. Our brains need to be cleansed of negative thoughts, they assert. The best cleansing compound is made of positive thoughts. If we think positively, we will feel and act positively. I've known a psychologist to provide the following prescription: "Read out loud the following affirmations. Visualize them. Increase your mind power which in turn changes your life. On each of 21 days, saturate your mind with these 21 visualizations":

1. I am OK.
2. I am worthwhile.
3. I am special.
4. I am one of a kind.
5. I belong—I am part of the universe.
6. I have great potential.
7. I am a responsible person.
8. I enjoy being myself.
9. I have a zest for living.
10. I feel warm and happy toward myself.
11. I approve of myself.
12. I feel warm and friendly toward others.
13. I can let others have whatever feelings they wish to have toward me without feeling hurt.
14. I look forward to new experiences with an inner confidence.
15. I see my mistakes as an opportunity for growing.
16. I accept criticism as information for my growing.
17. I do my own thinking and learn as I go.
18. Each decision I make is at that moment my best decision.
19. I willingly accept the consequences of my own behavior.
20. I am free to express both anger and joy.
21. I accept compliments without embarrassment.

But validation from within also has perilous insufficiencies. Such auto-suggestions are as apt to spawn heroic pride as they are spiritual strength, and typically they reveal a naive conception of those forces of evil that hold us in bondage. Self-validation offers some real help, but no lasting security.

The validation of our baptism.   The knowledge that validation by others or from within ourselves is ultimately inadequate could lead us to despair if an affirmation that validates for all time were not open to us. The God who gave us life and spiritual rebirth affirms us in a way that neither we nor our companions can ever do. Isaiah 43:1 says, "I have called you by name, you are mine." Knowing who we are depends finally on knowing *whose* we are.

Baptism makes me a somebody. I'm not just a number. I have a name that is special to me, and an identity within God's family. Baptism tells me that God is graciously disposed toward me. Baptism tells me that I count with God, and if I count with God, friend, I count! For God is in charge of this universe, the CEO—Chief Executive Officer! And if that boss says I'm OK, I'm OK!

Walking Wet

In times of greatest personal struggle and doubt Martin Luther often repeated the words, *"Baptizatus sum!"* ("I am baptized!") Like Luther, we can say, "Get going, forces of evil. Get going, devil. I don't belong to you. You can't win, because I belong to the God who is Victor. God has baptized me into the strong name of the divine. I bear the mark of that baptism for all time and claim the sustaining grace of God's power and victory in my life."

Victory always? Oh, no, not if we understand it as living in perpetual, glorious triumph. Baptism does not protect us from temptation or from sinning, even though the ultimate victory has been won. But it does link us eternally with the grace and power of God whereby we are again and again restored and strengthened—raised to new life.

Baptized Christians must fight the battle against sin daily, and still they face the fact of physical death. But because God has entered into a relationship with us in baptism, we are freed from the terror of sin, death, and the devil. For in baptism, God forgives sin, delivers from death and the devil, and gives everlasting life to all who believe what God has promised.

What is begun in baptism is a life of "walking wet" in the continuing struggle of a life of faith.

You Not Only Get Washed, You Die

Water is a source of life, cleansing, and refreshment. But water is also a potential killer. From early childhood we are warned that even a small amount of water can lead to a suffocating death.

In the baptismal imagery of Romans 6, we are buried with Christ by baptism into death. Going under water symbolizes the end of everything about our life that is less than what God intends for us. Coming up again symbolizes the beginning in us of something strange and new and hopeful—newness of life empowered by the God of our baptism.

What is begun in baptism is a continuing drama of death. I know that there are some forces in me that should die—again and again. There are fears and jealousies that plague me. They should die. There is self-pity, guilt, and pride. They should die. Indifference, apathy, and lust harass me. They should die. In short, there is a "me" that has died and needs continually to be put to death. In the language of the Scriptures, there is an "old Adam/Eve" in me that the apostle Paul called the "body of death." That old Adam/Eve that has been a part of me since birth should die—drowned through daily repentance as I continue to live out what it means to be buried by baptism into death.

Holy Baptism then is not just a onetime burial ceremony. The old Adam/Eve is infinitely more clever than the proverbial cat with nine lives. Whenever I sense that my old selfishness or my old adherence to false securities are still alive and kicking, that's a sign that the old Adam/Eve has not been finished off for good but is still present to plague and bully me. I know the old Adam/Eve has been defeated, but I also know that it remains annoyingly and lastingly pestiferous.

You Not Only Die, You Get Raised to New Life

Evangelical Christians dare to speak of baptism as death and follow the Scriptures in saying that daily repentance is the ongoing drowning that relates my baptism to my daily faith struggle. But lest I begin to claim too much credit and believe that my repentance is attributable to my growing moral muscle, the Scriptures also declare that even as Christ was raised from the dead by the glory of the Father, so too we walk in newness of life only through the grace of that "glory of the Father."

Our rising to new life in Christ by the glory of the Father is the dynamic that pulses through our repentance, and our repeated repentance fuels our resurrected life of holiness.

Baptism then is a death and resurrection drama that is the ever-pumping heart of our spirituality. We "walk wet" in the pilgrimage of faith. Baptism is the tap root that waters the tree of life growing within. What is begun in baptism is a beginning that has no ending. When we come to the end of our life, we need not fear our final death. We remember our baptism. With Christ, we have already gone through death once before, and we need not fear what we have already experienced.

Baptism—a birthing, a belonging, a beginning. How marvelous is the seeking, inexhaustible, and unmerited grace of God!

Can Searching for God Be Legitimate?

The pop spirituality of a few years ago declared, "I found it." From lapel pins to bumper stickers, the message became a passing craze. But a chorus of the pious countered with, "Don't say, 'I found it,' but instead 'God found me.' "

Sometimes a similar message is voiced in this way: "Our task is not to search for God, but rather to open ourselves to the reality of God's search for us." Sometimes it takes the form of a query: "Is 'decision theology' defensible?"

A gospel-centered spirituality is rooted in God's invasive grace, God's ceaseless pursuit of us as the gracious "hound of heaven." But I'm not ready to tear out of my Bible or explain away those passages that speak also of our search for God. The psalmist spoke also for me in the declaration, "As a hart longs for flowing streams, so longs my soul for thee, O God. My soul thirsts for God, for the living God" (Ps. 42:1-2).

I'm troubled more by those who insist we choose which position is "right" than by the paradox of saying both postures should be given their full biblical legitimacy. I'm troubled, for example, by those who want to define spirituality solely in terms of our search for a transcendent fulfillment of our human nature. If spirituality has to do only with our reaching out and responding to that basic, mysterious human yearning for the infinite, then in what sense is spirituality related to our baptism? I refuse both horns of the dilemma—being unwilling to ignore the reality of an inner hunger for God, but adamantly disallowing the separation of spirituality from sacramental grace in baptism.

I prefer a definition of spirituality that takes into account both the intrinsic love of God for a fallen humanity *and* a human nature that is called and empowered to grow in the image of God. Being "dead in trespasses and sin" does not mean that there is not a restlessness within (of God's implantation) that only God can satisfy. However, it takes many of us an inordinate length of time, much groping, and countless dead ends before we realize that we have been fleeing from a pursuing God who wills only our good, but who can give us that "good" only as we die to "good," as we customarily define it. So we both hunger for God and flee from God. We remain restless until we find peace with God, yet typically we seek that peace by means of idols of our own devising.

Toward a Definition of Spirituality

In his book *Gravity and Grace*, Joseph Sittler said, "The word *spirituality*—the power, presence, dynamics of the spirit—is not a definable reality."[1] I quite agree. At best, one can assemble building blocks that provide hints and helps.

I define spirituality as:

- that by which one is sustained inwardly when all external supports give way;
- that by which a person connects with and surrenders to a force beyond his or her own consciousness which gives meaning, freedom, and joy;
- knowing and trusting that anchor, that rock, that fortress which provides security, refuge, and haven amid life's storms and stresses;
- being the new person that we have become through the waters of our baptism;
- a holistic, lifelong response to the grace of God shown us most perfectly in Christ through whose merits we are fashioned into his likeness through the change-agentry of the Holy Spirit;
- not an escapist asceticism that seeks to flee the body, history, and the body politic, but a life-embracing living-in-depth; the

day-to-day living out of the relationship with God which we
have in Christ;

- not morality of the sort that leads to restrictive, narrowed
  existence, but the freeing impulses growing out of true and full
  acceptance of our humanity under God;
- being sustained by a Word and sacrament ministry within the
  church;
- awe before the mystery of life and our humble answer to the
  inconceivable surprise of living;
- belonging to God's people;
- trusting God;
- a Christ-centered orientation to God, nature, society, and self;
- love that is accepted, expressed, lived, and shared;
- plugging along through the nitty-gritty of life fueled by a hope-
  fulness that knows how the story is finally going to end, and
  persistently holding to the disputed notion that the one who
  was before all and in whom all things cohere is the same one
  who is already now with us on the way.

Martin Luther, in a work prepared in 1527, insisted that "everything our body does outwardly and physically is in reality and in
name done spiritually if God's Word is added to it and it is done
in faith. Nothing can be so material, fleshly, or outward but that
it becomes spiritual when it is done in the Word and in faith. 'The
spiritual' is nothing more than what is done in us and by us through
the Spirit and faith, whether the object with which we are dealing
is physical or spiritual."[2] I understand Luther to mean that the
spiritually minded person does not differ from the materially minded
person chiefly in thinking about different things, but in thinking
about the same things differently.

I am aware that, in the minds of some, spirituality gets identified
with such diverse things as parapsychological phenomena, magic,
witchcraft, various cults, the occult, astrology, theosophy, demon-
ology, hallucinogenic drugs, altered states of consciousness, visions,
locutions, levitation, bilocation, moments of ecstatic rapture, other-
worldliness, and the like.

Others identify spirituality with such charismatic phenomena as
utterance of wisdom, working of miracles, prophecy, gifts of healing,

discernment of spirits, various kinds of tongues, the interpretation of tongues, the utterance of knowledge, and deliverance from demons.

Still others use *spirituality* as a catch-all term embracing such fads as aerobic "Jesus-ercise" for pious overeaters, pumping iron, jogging, health foods, disciplinary morality, and so on.

Probably because of such wildly varied associations and connotations, many people respond with skepticism, if not fear, to things "spiritual." Some frankly believe the term to be beyond rehabilitation.

In my experience, I have found church members curiously content to sing: "I ask no dream, no prophet ecstasies, no sudden rending of the veil of clay, no angel visitant, no op'ning skies; but take the dimness of my soul away."[3] That hymn is interestingly selective in what it seeks as a spiritual experience: *not* dreams, prophetic ecstasies, angelic visitations, etc., *but* "take the dimness of my soul away . . . wean my heart from earthly things . . . make me love you as I ought to love." I wonder: Is there anything more or less spiritual about the second list than the first? Is it simply spiritual modesty that prescribes what gets on the OK-to-ask-for list? Or are we presuming to tell God what specific spiritual experiences we will and will not welcome?

Some evangelical Christians are suspicious of the whole concept of spirituality. They say that the traditional, medieval view of spirituality and its accompanying disciplines are at odds with a truly evangelical, grace-centered emphasis. Reformation theology, they go on to say, has appropriately challenged all mysticisms of ascent to God in which the focus falls on the human struggle for perfection.

For many mystics and champions of spirituality, union with God comes at the top of a ladder of purification, usually after prolonged and serious commitment to spiritual disciplines. The theological objection to this kind of spirituality is that it makes union with God a *goal* to be achieved, while the gospel makes union with God through baptism the *starting point* of Christian life. Through baptism, we are united with God; we subsequently live out this union through the death of daily repentance and through resurrection to newness of life in Jesus Christ.

Gospel-centered Christians expect always to remain pilgrims, growing (and needing to grow) spiritually. But they believe that their ongoing sinfulness in not a sign of spiritual retardation, but of the fact that God is not finished with them yet. They insist that one does not have to complete a spiritual marathon to have full communion with God.

Some gospel-centered Christians are ready to dismiss all talk of spirituality. They see it as simply another manifestation of that resilient "old Adam/Eve" that rises ever anew to grasp *for* God, when it should die so that a new self can freely commune *with* God. "Marvel not," they say, "at the rise of spirituality. Consider only that the works of the flesh are many and varied as it seeks life on its own terms."

Yet others point out that what we are experiencing today as a resurgence of interest in spirituality may be little more than a change of terminology. Some of the topics now included under the rubric of spirituality used to be called discipleship, stewardship, or ethics.

I return to the Sittler quotation on spirituality. Precisely because we grapple here with that which "is not a definable reality," we need to exercise discernment.

A Call for Discernment

There have long been pockets of interest in diverse sorts of supernaturalism. Before 1960, they remained very much on the fringe of Western culture. Such assorted interests as Transcendental Meditation, yoga, Eastern mysticism, Satan worship, Scientology, Mind Dynamics, spiritism, out-of-body experiences, reincarnation, Theosophy, and the like have seemed to challenge both naturalism on the one hand and the Judeo-Christian tradition on the other.

Blendings of non-Christian religions, the realm of the occult, and the "milder" interests having to do with health and ecological concerns, futurism, holistic medicine, alternative life-styles, anti-nuclear weapons demonstrations, and the like have, since the 1960s, moved more into the mainstream of American consciousness where they have become popularly known as "New Age."

Critiques of the many and various movements collectively iden-tified as New Age have been made elsewhere, and it goes beyond my purpose to review those assessments here. But the New Age phenomenon does provide evidence that there are great spiritual stirrings in our time. And I want to emphasize that just because a particular movement challenges our culture's naturalistic worldview, that does not automatically make it an ally of the Christian faith.

A New Age worldview holds that metaphysical ignorance, not sinful rebellion against God, is the root of humanity's woes. What is needed, they declare, is a special knowledge that is brought about by psycho-spiritual techniques that rid consciousness of the fragmenting effects of reason and the crippling effects of inadequate belief. Enlightenment, self-realization, cosmic consciousness, and New Age transformation all speak of supernaturalism, to be sure, but not one that can be uncritically embraced by gospel-centered Christians. It takes careful discernment not to be swept up by any and all forces that find their commonality simply as warriors against the naturalism of Western culture.

A Personalized Scenario

A gospel-centered spirituality appropriately addresses the needs of a wide variety of spiritual stirrings in our time. It makes connections with the many and various ways these stirrings are expressed. Perhaps this chapter so far has been too theoretical—too left-brained. How about a scenario that is more personalized? Consider these vignettes drawn from real life:

• A young man hardened by years of neglecting the church finds himself crying during the celebration of the Lord's Supper at a weekend retreat for singles.

• A physician schooled in hard-nosed science puts aside her skepticism while attending a Cursillo retreat and entertains thoughts about things that cannot be measured but nonetheless press upon her as being very real.

• An addict in his craving says he's tried all else and wonders if God can deliver him from his addiction.

• A retired couple decides that their abundant creaturely comforts do not provide satisfaction, and they become involved with several volunteer ministries and justice programs.

• A mother finds her identity shaken to the foundations when her youngest child leaves home, and she takes up a mid-life search that focuses on questions with spiritual themes.

These are not imaginary persons. One could add to the list countless more examples. What are they but a sampling of the immense number of people who have an authentic hunger, a feeling deep inside that something is missing? In the next chapter I will discuss four basic ways in which this hunger takes shape in the form of spirituality.

2 Four Types of Spirituality

A man found an eagle's egg and put it in the nest of a backyard hen. The eaglet hatched with the brood of chicks and grew up with them.

All his life the eagle did what the backyard chickens did, thinking he was a backyard chicken. He scratched the earth for worms and insects. He clucked and cackled. And he thrashed his wings and flew a few feet into the air.

Years passed and the eagle grew very old. One day he saw a magnificent bird far above him in the cloudless sky. It glided in a graceful majesty among the powerful wind currents, with scarcely a beat of its strong golden wings.

The old eagle looked up in awe. "Who's that?" he asked.

"That's the eagle, the king of the birds," said one of the backyard chickens. "He belongs to the sky. We belong to the earth—we're chickens."

So the eagle lived and died a chicken, for that's what he thought he was.[1]

Spirituality is of interest to those who know they come, as it were, from a "spiritual egg." Human beings are spiritual creatures. God has fashioned us with a capacity for interrelationship with the Almighty. The word *spirit* comes from a word meaning "breath." The God-given breath of life is that fragile yet effective channel through which we seek God, but through which we come to discover that God is the seeker and we are the sought.

When one takes an analytical look at spirituality, such as we will do in this chapter, one is struck by the rich diversity that exists. This should not surprise us. Just as no two sets of fingerprints or voice prints are exactly alike, God's preference for uniqueness is also demonstrated in spirituality.

How can one meaningfully describe the great variety that exists in spirituality? The most helpful way is to try to identify general patterns. We must remember that to generalize is to distort; to group together is to overlook some differences that matter. But with that caution in mind, it nonetheless seems helpful to work with a typology of spirituality.

A Phenomenology of Spirituality

By surveying the emphases of various Christian spiritual masters and describing spiritual practices as objectively as possible, it is possible to fashion a phenomenology of spirituality; that is, to characterize the visible patterns of Christian spirituality.

Urban T. Holmes has written A *History of Christian Spirituality* (Westminster, 1984) in which he provides two scales and four types of orthodox Christian spirituality. John H. Westerhoff has worked with Holmes in detailing the typology. While visiting with Westerhoff at Duke Divinity School, he shared with me a "Circle of Sensibility" schema, which I find most useful in characterizing spirituality today.

Before presenting that schema I wish to say that since 1984, when my wife and I first began giving spirituality workshops, it has been my experience that participants are more effectively drawn into this material if they first have been invited to identify their own preferred spirituality type. This can be done by means of an inventory that I have devised and field-tested for several years.

The inventory has several advantages. It is brief and can be given and scored in a relatively short time. When given to groups of 20 or more, it has never failed to identify at least three and usually all four types of spirituality.

While participants have seldom quarreled with the results of their being "typed," I make no claims for the scientific validity or reliability of this instrument. Right now I am less interested in generating statistics than in helping people become more aware and respectful of the prevailing diversity of spirituality types.[2]

As you complete the following inventory, keep in mind that there are no right or wrong answers. I am convinced that these are all legitimate types of Christian spirituality.

The forced-choice options may at times discomfort you as you feel yourself drawn almost equally to both alternatives, or know yourself to prefer at different times either of the options. It usually works best to go with your first, immediate inclination.

Spirituality Types

Spiritual preferences and habits come in patterns, in combinations. Described below are four patterns you can use to study your preferred spirituality style. This exercise is not a test. There are no right or wrong patterns. Which pattern best describes you? Read across the page and circle that sentence, phrase, or word in each coupling that comes closest to describing your preferences or habits. Choose only one of each pairing in this forced-choice inventory.

A

I prefer to think of God as revealed and knowable.	I prefer to think of God as hidden in mystery.
I prefer to focus on the similarities that exist between God and God's creatures.	I prefer to focus on the radical differences between God and God's creatures.
Concepts, images, and symbols help to make God real to me.	Only dark, silent love can comprehend the incomprehensible God.
The good news requires me to use my intellect in an affirmative way.	The good news is that God can be experienced in a relationship of mystical love.
Meditation on God's Word leads me to illumination of God's will.	Contemplation of God's Being leads me to union with God.

Which word or phrase in each across-the-page pairing appeals to you more? Think what the word or phrase means rather than how it looks or how it sounds.

B

Detachment	Attachment
Spending time with God	Doing things for God
Letting go	Taking charge
Seeing ordinary things as God might see them	Desiring the extraordinary to experience God
Floating	Swimming
Seeking the God of consolations	Seeking the consolations of God

Continue this inventory of spirituality types by determining which pattern describes you best. Circle one of each coupling, reading across the page.

C

What the church most needs is better sermons and study groups.	What the church most needs is more experiential worship and small-group relations.
I enjoy thinking about God and the things of God.	I enjoy feeling the presence and caring of God.
The illumination of the mind is central to spirituality.	The illumination of the heart is central to spirituality.
God has a good path into my life through my will.	God has a good path into my life through my intuition.
I value truth.	I value feelings.

A final section follows. Continue the same practice of choosing one preference from each coupling.

D

Devoted	Determined
I more often let my heart rule my head.	I more often let my head rule my heart.
Touching	Convincing
I usually value sentiment more than logic.	I usually value logic more than sentiment.
Compassion	Foresight
Whenever possible, I try to be a person of real feeling.	Whenever possible, I try to be a consistently reasonable person.

Scoring Guide

Count the number of sentences you circled in the left column of Section A and add that number to the number of words and phrases you circled in the right column of Section B.
Write that total here: ⎯⎯⎯⎯⎯

Count the number of sentences you circled in the right column of Section A and add that number to the number of words and phrases you circled in the left column of Section B.
Write that total here: ⎯⎯⎯⎯⎯
(The sum of the two "totals" should be 11.)

If the number in your first blank is a 6 or 7, circle: **K−**
If the number in your first blank is an 8 or 9, circle: **K**
If the number in your first blank is a 10 or 11, circle: **K+**
If the number in your first blank is 1 to 5, simply proceed with your scoring.

If the number in your second blank is a 6 or 7, circle: **A−**
If the number in your second blank is an 8 or 9, circle: **A**
If the number in your second blank is a 10 or 11, circle: **A+**
(You should have either a K or an A scoring, not one of each.)

Next count the number of sentences or words you circled in the left column of Section C and add that number to the number of items you circled in the right column of Section D.

Write that total here: _____

Count the number of sentences or words you circled in the right column of Section C and add that number to the number of items you circled in the left column of Section D.

Write that total here: _____

(The sum of these two "totals" should be 11.)

If the number in your third blank is a 6 or 7, circle: **M–**
If the number in your third blank is an 8 or 9, circle: **M**
If the number in your third blank is a 10 or 11, circle: **M+**
If the number in your third blank is a 1 to 5, simply proceed with your scoring.

If the number in your fourth blank is a 6 or 7, circle: **H–**
If the number in your fourth blank is an 8 or 9, circle: **H**
If the number in your fourth blank is a 10 or 11, circle: **H+**
(You should have either an M or an H scoring, not one of each.)

Circle below the composite of the two letter scores you circled above.

K–/M–	K–/M	K–/M+	K–/H–	K–/H	K–/H+
K/M–	K/M	K/M+	K/H–	K/H	K/H+
K+/M	K+/M	K+/M+	K+/H–	K+/H	K+/H+
A–/M–	A–/M	A–/M+	A–/H–	A–/H	A–/H+
A/M–	A/M	A/M+	A/H–	A/H	A/H+
A+/M–	A+/M	A+/M+	A+/H–	A+/H	A+/H+

Note first on the "Circle of Sensibility" schema found on p. 36, the two axes. The north–south scale is an "orientation/ends" scale. The upper hemisphere represents those who seek illumination of the mind in their desire to know God. Those in the southern hemisphere seek illumination of the heart, desiring to have an affective rather than speculative relationship with God.

The east–west scale is a "technique/means" scale indicating the preferred ways and means of going about the spiritual life. Here we have two Greek words historically used to contrast styles of spirituality.

TYPES OF CHRISTIAN SPIRITUALITY*

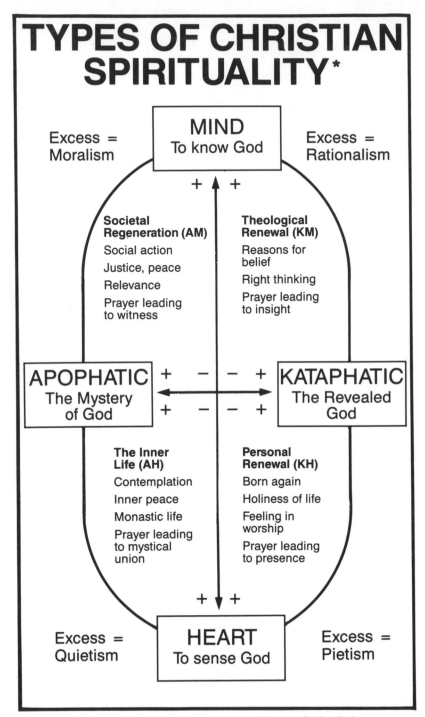

Excess =
Moralism

MIND
To know God

Excess =
Rationalism

+ ↑ +

Societal Regeneration (AM)

Social action

Justice, peace

Relevance

Prayer leading to witness

Theological Renewal (KM)

Reasons for belief

Right thinking

Prayer leading to insight

APOPHATIC
The Mystery of God

+ − − +
← →
+ − − +

KATAPHATIC
The Revealed God

The Inner Life (AH)

Contemplation

Inner peace

Monastic life

Prayer leading to mystical union

Personal Renewal (KH)

Born again

Holiness of life

Feeling in worship

Prayer leading to presence

+ ↓ +

Excess =
Quietism

HEART
To sense God

Excess =
Pietism

*Based on "A Circle of Sensibility" from *A History of Christian Spirituality* by Urban Holmes III. Copyright © 1980 by Urban Holmes III. Reprinted by permission of Harper & Row, Publishers, Inc.

Kataphatic means to engage the revealed God by attempting to image God through the senses. The Greek word *kataphatikos* means "affirmative." Kataphatic mysticism, the *via affirmativa*, emphasizes the similarity that exists between God and creatures and recommends the use of concepts, images, and symbols as a way of meditating with a God who is revealed and knowable.

The Greek word *apophatikos* means "negative." Apophatic mysticism, the *via negativa*, emphasizes the radical difference between God and creatures. God is best reached, therefore, by negation, forgetting, and unknowing in sensory darkness without the support of concepts, images, and symbols. This mystical tradition emphasizes that God cannot be known by the intellect or appropriated by any of the senses.[3] Only dark, silent love can comprehend the ever-greater God. God is mystery and can be experienced only through the way of infused contemplation.

James Finley, writing in *The Awakening Call*, expressed the apophatic tradition is this manner: "The contemplative way is that of naked faith, through which one is led in poverty and great longing beyond all concepts and images into a deep hidden knowledge of our union with God in Christ."[4]

Anthony de Mello wrote in *One Minute Wisdom:*

"Every word, every image used for God is a distortion more than a description."
"Then how does one speak of God?"
"Through Silence."
"Why, then, do you speak in words?"
At that the Master laughed uproariously. He said, "When I speak, you mustn't listen to the words, my dear. Listen to the Silence."[5]

Theologically, many of us have no trouble saying that God is at once both revealed and hidden, but in the interplay between revelation and mystery, mystery typically is underplayed.

Precisely because God is both revealed and hidden, one might expect to find no exclusive or pure samples of these two orthodox ways of spirituality. Any one type of mysticism always contains some elements from the other type. Genuine Christian mysticism holds the similarity/dissimilarity distinction together in widely varied arrays of creative tension.

So we have a north–south set of hemispheres and an east–west set, creating four quadrants or types of spirituality: kataphatic or apophatic; mind or heart.

One other perspective needs to be presented before we begin our sequential review of each quadrant. According to Westerhoff, each school of spirituality should be seen to be in dialectical tension with the school in the opposite diagonal quadrant of the circle. Thus K/M folks need to be complemented by A/H adherents to prevent them from falling outside the circle of sensibility into the excess or heresy of rationalism. You'll note on the schema that each quadrant has an excess indicated: rationalism, pietism, quietism, and mor- alism.

(If, in scoring your inventory, you came up with a "plus" figure, you may wish to assess more carefully whether your spirituality may not be approaching the excess that is noted.)

Now to the first of the four quadrants.

Apophatic/Heart Spirituality (A/H)

We begin with the lower left quadrant, the A/H (Apophatic/ Heart) type. Remember, you should not press unduly the details of these descriptions. Get the central tendency. Discover the core characteristics. In following Holmes/Westerhoff, I shall risk specific examples from history, not all of which shall be equally fitting.

For samples of an apophatic/heart spirituality, we look to the monastic and ascetic movements marked by a disciplined pursuit of an inner consciousness of God. These persons prefer to live a contemplative life away from the world. Intuition is dominant; feelings are primary. They desire much prayer and quiet in worship. Contemplative prayer leading to mystical union is the means and goal.

The excess is quietism, the tendency toward neglect of culture, and excessive concern for absorption into God.

This spirituality is directed inward. Overwhelmed or bewildered by life's struggles and/or put off by an excessive rationalism in their religion, A/H types strive for a union with God that lies beneath or beyond the outward.

Contemplation provides a sense of rest, inner peace, and private solace apart from the tumultuousness of life round about. Matthew

Fox has written these words that would undoubtedly be applauded by A/H adherents:

Something drastic has happened to words and to language in the West.

Words today come cheap. When a president can say "I am not a crook" and people learn that means "I am a crook," and when "peace-making efforts" mean invasions of war, the people become suspicious of words—and rightly so. When the most significant psychological thinker of our time, Sigmund Freud, points out that words are very often a cover-up and that more truth is to be learned from dreams or even slips of the tongue than from controlled speech, those who preach the Word are going to speak to ever-dwindling audiences. . . . I do not deny that a theology of the Word is rich and full of meaning to those who have had the luxury of studying its long historical development. But as a pedagogical method, it begins with two strikes against it because our culture is *sick of words*. What we want is the nonword, the unword, the silence, the touch, the dance, the music— in short, a new word and a new language that the mystic who rejects society's language eventually comes to utter. My well-trained Prot-estant theologian friends tell me: "But all this is implied in a theology of the Word." To which I reply: "The average person does not know this. Why make your job harder than it need be?" Besides, despite verbal protestations by theologians, many Protestant worship services remain profoundly and dismally wordy, ill at ease with silence, dance, mime and other, deeper words.[6]

If you find it difficult to relate to these statements by Matthew Fox, don't automatically reject this apophatic/heart mode. You may find it easier to identify with a prayer by a pastor who, in my judgment, was somewhere within this quadrant, when he shared these words at a retreat:

Lord, I'm tired.

I'm tired of being busy.

I'm tired of work that keeps pushing me to do more and more and more.

I'm tired of religious activities and retreats and continuing education courses that often leave me more worn out than rested.

Lord, teach me how to relax in your presence
  to rest in your care
  to breath in the balm of your Spirit.

Open me to your reassuring promises
    to the discernment of your will and way in the clutter of my
    mixed values and uncertain priorities.

Lord, be my resting place
  my peace
  my shalom
  my eternal salvation
      through Christ, my Savior and Lord.

Amen.

Eldon L. Olson has provided additional help in his essay, "Spirituality: Christian Varieties from a Lutheran Perspective."[7] I will be using some of his categories and commentary as an overlay on the Westerhoff/Holmes schema.

Olson speaks of four forms of spirituality. The one most compatible with the A/H quadrant is the one he terms "The Spirituality of the Inner Life." This spirituality is directed toward an inner change of life, an inner quest for a nature that is conformable to the nature of Christ.

St. Bernard of Clairvaux, the great ascetic and churchman of the 12th century, stands out as one of the foremost proponents of the spirituality of the inner life. Although he discounted the importance of mystical union with God, his words betray the central concern for the pilgrimage of the Christian to ever-greater heights of self-mortification and spiritual illumination. Thomas à Kempis's little classic, *The Imitation of Christ* (the most widely circulated volume of Christian spirituality ever written) is also predominantly of this type.

Classic proponents of an A/H spirituality see the Christian as a person on a pilgrimage toward salvation and union with God. Distractions of the flesh are barriers requiring discipline and self-denial. Ideally, a spiritual director guides the ascent, in the popular image of the ladder, to ever-greater heights of purgation and illumination as the person aspires to oneness with God, to absorption into the mystery of the Trinity itself. Few would claim the attainment of this ultimate goal, but whole lifetimes were and are spent in its pursuit.

Of late, elements of Transcendental Meditation, Zen Buddhism, and depth psychology have been blended with Christian traditions to provide a strange marriage of methods and models that add variety to the contemporary manifestation of this type of spirituality. It may be argued that concerns for self-realization and self-actualization— indeed, the whole turn inward so evident in our culture today— has parallel elements with the monastic and ascetic movements.

Since the apophatic tradition of mysticism sees less value in linear, propositional talk, perhaps illustrative stories are a more fruitful and faithful way to depict the essence of this type of spirituality.

From *The Song of the Bird* by Anthony de Mello comes this vignette:

> In the last century, a tourist from the States visited the famous Polish rabbi, Hafez Hayyim.
> He was astonished to see that the rabbi's home was only a simple room filled with books. The only furniture was a table and a bench.
> "Rabbi, where is your furniture?" asked the tourist.
> "Where is yours?" replied Hafez.
> "Mine? But I'm only a visitor here."
> "So am I," said the rabbi.[8]

Here's another I like which I've entitled "Spirituality and the Talkative Lover."

> A lover pressed his suit unsuccessfully for many months, suffering the atrocious pains of rejection.
> Finally his sweetheart yielded. "Come to such and such a place, at such and such an hour," she said to him.
> At that time and place the lover finally found himself seated beside his beloved. He then reached into his pocket and pulled out a sheaf of love letters that he had written to her over the past months. They were passionate letters, expressing the pain he felt and his burning desire to experience the delights of love and union. He began to read them to his beloved. The hours passed by but still he read on and on.
> Finally the woman said, "What kind of a fool are you? These letters are all about me and your longing for me. Well, here I am sitting with you at last and you are lost in your stupid letters."

"Here I am with you," says God, "and you keep reflecting about me in your head, talking about me with your tongue, and searching for me in your books. When will you shut up and see?"[9]

In John 1:14 we read: "And the Word became flesh and dwelt among us." What I need to do is stop my frantic efforts to change flesh back into words. Words, words, words. Why is it that we religious professionals typically have trouble with the incarnation?

Spirituality of an apophatic/heart mode may at times manifest itself as serenity to accept what cannot be changed.

A man who took great pride in his lawn found himself with a large crop of dandelions. He tried every method he knew to get rid of them. Still they plagued him.

Finally he wrote the Department of Agriculture. He enumerated all the things he had tried and closed his letter with the question: "What shall I do now?"

In due course the reply came: "We suggest you learn to love them."[10]

Loving resignation belongs to A/H spirituality.

To the disciples who wanted to know what sort of meditation he practiced each morning in the garden, the Master said, "When I look *carefully*, I see the rose bush in full bloom."

"Why would one have to look carefully to see the rose bush?" they asked.

"Lest one see not the rose bush," said the Master, "but one's preconception of it."[11]

In my graduate studies in communication at Northwestern University, I took a number of courses in general semantics. One of the major principles of general semantics is, "The map is not the territory." The word is not the reality it seeks to depict and to which it points.

The disciples were absorbed in a discussion of the dictum: "Those who know do not say; those who say do not know." When the Master entered, they asked him exactly what the words meant.

Said the Master, "Which of you knows the fragrance of a rose?" All of them knew. Then he said, "Put it into words."

All of them were silent.[12]

From early on, monks have fled to the desert that they might more fully pursue self-discipline and self-knowledge in the "universities of its solitude." We ought not to think that the monks' yearning for isolation and solitude was merely a desire for a return to a more unencumbered life—pastoral peacefulness over against the artificial life of the cities. While we may grant some desire to escape the bustle and busyness of life, it must be acknowledged that solitude has its own positive valence and attractiveness as a favored habitat for a spirituality beyond words.

Thomas Merton explained it this way. Christianity, he wrote, is essentially a religion of the Word of God. It is easy to forget that this Word first of all emerges out of silence. Underlying the search for interior solitude is the basic posturing of self so as best to hear that Word when it is spoken.[13]

Don't you agree, for example, that to do justice to the mystery and joy of Easter with the stale words of human speech is difficult? Perhaps it should be harder to preach on Easter morning than it appears to be for most of us preacher types.

Adherents of an A/H spirituality will likely be attracted to such spiritual disciplines as solitude, fasting, simplicity, and spiritual direction. Those four spiritual disciplines are but illustrative. A/H folk have no monopoly on them, nor will all A/H adherents defend their usefulness to a similar extent. That leads to the assertion that may be generalized to cover all references to disciplines. Choice is of utmost importance for spiritual growth. Only when religion becomes fanaticism or sublimation to a dangerous degree is it so compelling that one does not need to make a choice. Apart from fanatical religion, which I cannot defend, external religious behavior and inner spiritual disciplines are matters for deliberation and choice.

One final story before we leave the A/H quadrant.

I used to be stone deaf.
I would see people stand up and go through all kinds of gyrations.
    They called it dancing.
    It looked absurd to me
      —until one day, I, too,
      heard the music!

I fail to understand why saints, mystics, and lovers behave the way
   they do.
And so I'm waiting for the day when I, too,
   shall hear the music to which they move.[14]

Kataphatic/Mind Spirituality (K/M)

We move next to that quadrant diagonal from the A/H, namely
the K/M, the Kataphatic/Mind, or Speculative/Imaging type.

Here the intellect is dominant. Sensate thinking is to the fore.
There is involvement with the world, though more concern to
understand than to change it. Mental prayer leading to insight is
the goal of meditation. Better sermons and study groups is the desire
brought to the worship arena.

What Olson calls "The Spirituality of Theological Renewal" I
see as fitting essentially within this quadrant. In this spirituality,
one looks outside oneself in the awareness that happiness, peace,
blessedness, and righteousness are neither present nor potential as
an inner achievement. Be less focused on self, one's own volition
and activities and achievements, and more on the disposition and
activity of God, especially as that becomes manifest in the Christ
event.

Peter Taylor Forsyth speaks as one would out of this quadrant:

Do not tell people how they ought to feel toward Christ. It is just
what they ought that they cannot do. Preach a Christ that will make
them feel as they ought. That is objective preaching. The tendency
and fashion of the present moment is all in the direction of subjec-
tivity. People welcome sermons of a more or less psychological kind,
which go into the analysis of the soul or of society. They will listen
gladly to sermons on character-building, for instance; and in the result
they will get to think of nothing else but their own character. They
will be the builders of their own character; which is a fatal thing.
Learn to commit your soul and the building of it to One who can
keep it and build it as you never can. Attend then to Christ, the
Holy Spirit, the kingdom, and the cause, and he will look after your
soul.[15]

There is little focus on personal piety, on inner reflection, on
the personal pursuit of moral righteousness. Such a one would rather

say: "Christ has done for me and to me what I could not do for myself. I look less to my own death through self-mortification and more to the death of Christ on the cross—a death which *is* the death of my old self."

Spiritual transformation is not something *we* do; rather, faith lays hold of what God has done and is doing through the renewing work of the Holy Spirit. You want to see the raging battle between the forces of good and evil? Look not to your own inner struggles, but to the cross, for there the primary conflict is waged—there the victory is achieved. Recognize that the frantic frenzy of piety and righteous works may well be the old self resisting its own destruction by that objective event of God's doing. The spiritual identity of the believer is fixed by that cross event and the believer is freed thereby for a life of service and love, of prayer, self-discipline, and alms-giving.

No spiritual director is needed except the living Word and the Spirit that interprets Christ.

No higher state of spirituality is given except by the one gift of grace available to everyone, not just the spiritually elite.

No spiritual response is salvific except faith, faith being both primal and primary.

Pauline and Augustinian traditions nurture such a spirituality. The spirituality of theological renewal encompasses Luther, though one may find in Luther's voluminous writings passages illustrative of all four quadrants. Such diverse modern theologians as Barth, Bultmann, Tillich, and Niebuhr elaborate themes belonging centrally to the spirituality of theological renewal.

St. Ignatius of Loyola, another 16th-century figure, stands predominantly in this kataphatic/mind tradition, though I have heard Jesuit-trained priests challenge the placement. He would be an excellent counterbalance for those prone to reduce spirituality to ecstatic experience and to deny the intellect its needs and rights in the mystical life. His *Spiritual Exercises* have played a significant role in Roman Catholic spirituality. For more than 400 years they have fed the spiritual lives of countless Jesuits. In the 1920s, Pope Pius IX declared St. Ignatius the "celestial patron of spiritual exercises" and recommended practice of his exercises to all.

At first glance, the exercises might appear to be nothing more than a series of meditations and contemplations on the life, death, and resurrection of Jesus Christ, interspersed with Ignatian parables, considerations, rules, and directives. What is unique about them is the methodical and explicit way Ignatius goes about assisting others in their spiritual journeying. The exercises are explicitly Christocentric, which might give those insistent on Holy Spirit terminology, as the primary language of spirituality, some cause for second thoughts.

When kataphatic/mind spirituality becomes excessive, you have the heresy of rationalism, exaggerated concern for reason and right thinking, formalistic dogmatism, propositional specificity about God and all God's ways with us.

Two short stories belong to this quadrant. The first I've entitled "Spirituality, Dogma, and Truth."

> I could hardly believe my eyes when I saw the name of the shop:
> THE TRUTH SHOP.
> It was just where I wanted to be.
>
> The saleswoman was very polite: "What type of truth do you wish to purchase," she asked, "partial or whole?"
>
> "Why, the whole truth, of course." No deceptions for me, no rationalizations. I wanted my truth plain and unadulterated.
>
> She waved me on to another side of the store.
>
> The saleswoman there pointed to the price tag. "The price is very high, sir," she warned.
>
> "What is it?" I asked, determined to get the whole truth, no matter what it cost.
>
> "Your security, sir," she answered.
>
> I came away with a heavy heart.
> I still need the safety of my unquestioned beliefs.[16]

Then there's the story of a pastor who was undoubtedly operating out of a K/M mode of spirituality. I've entitled it "How K/M Spirituality Handles Criticism."

A monkey up a tree hurled a coconut at the head of a Pastor.
The Pastor picked it up,
> drank the milk,
> ate the flesh,
> made a bowl from the shell,
and said: "Thank you for your criticism of me."[17]

Those whose spirituality is of the K/M sort may be especially attracted to such disciplines as journaling, study and reflection, and meditation in contrast to contemplation. I want to emphasize that my selection of these three exercises to highlight in conjunction with our review of the kataphatic/mind spirituality is again quite arbitrary. Though a case could easily be made that a speculative, imaging person might be drawn, for example, to the diary character of journaling, there are features of journaling as taught by Ira Progoff that border or bridge to the apophatic if, in fact, they do not belong there. That's just a reminder word to help keep our simple schema from becoming overly simplistic.

Kataphatic/Heart Spirituality (K/H)

I want to move next to the Kataphatic/Heart (K/H) mode of spirituality, the lower right quadrant. It is still kataphatic, still engaging the senses through constructs, words, images, and the like, but allowing the affect to dominate. These are the sensate folk who want to feel their religion. Some, if not most, are suspicious of doctrinal formalism. They are calling the church away from a stiff and staid spiritual intellectualism.

While kataphatics of the mind may charge, "My doctrine is purer than yours," kataphatics of the heart may counter with, "My walk with the Lord is closer than yours."

K/H adherents typically insist on an outward expression of an inner change. They search for an experiential identity in Christ that transforms and becomes evident in a Christian life-style. They say: commitment to Christ is transforming and will be revealed in the holiness of the believer; otherwise, they say, conversion is suspect.

Olson has identified an understanding of Christian spirituality that he calls "The Spirituality of Personal Renewal." I would locate this primarily within the K/H quadrant.

Those who favor the K/H type are different from those who advocate a spirituality of the inner life in that they accept no isolation from society. They seek, rather, to transform it and are apt to provide an enormous force for evangelism and social action. Also, they do not elevate the human soul as if spirituality were but a slice of the total human pie. They call for a transformation of the whole person, demonstrable in every way within a social context.

Pietist movements through the years most vividly portray this mode of spirituality. To the pietist, the essence of Christianity has to do with a conversion event marked by utter repentance and renewal, after which one attains a sense of intimacy with God that at once provides both a personal experience of the assurance of salvation and empowerment by the Holy Spirit for combating the forces of evil in one's self and in the world.

Although accused of emotionalism and subjectivism, pietists perceive the gospel in terms of a well-developed theological method. Puritanism belongs here. E. Glenn Hinson writes:

> Puritans were to Protestantism what contemplatives and ascetics were to the medieval church. . . . Where monks sought sainthood in monasteries, Puritans sought it everywhere—in homes, schools, town halls, shops as well as churches. . . . Like the monks, they were zealous of heart religion manifested in transformation of life and manners. Impatient with halfway commitments, they kindled fires for unreserved, enthusiastic embracing of the covenant.[18]

Classical Lutheran pietism sought to restore a dimension of depth to personal religious life through a living encounter with the living Lord. Preoccupied with the regeneration of persons, it occupied itself as well with the renewal of the church. It sought to revive a certain apostolic simplicity that centered in the love each member had for the other. There was passion for a congruence of confession and character, of profession and practice. This congruence was to be *seen* in the lives of persons and congregations. The end product of a good theology is not just correctly formulated propositions of the faith, they assert, but an incarnation in lives formed by the faith, the hope, and the love of Jesus Christ. Philip Spener (1635–1705) said: "The Reformation begun by Luther is far from completed as far as it regards life and morality."[19]

Frank C. Senn, writing of Lutheran spirituality, adds:

Folk piety was deepened in Norway by the controversial career of the lay preacher, Hans Nielsen Hauge (1771–1824), and in Finland by the similar career of the lay preacher, Pauvo Routsalainen (1777–1852). Pietist leaders in Sweden included Henrik Schartau (1757–1825), who laid great stress on the church's worship and whose catechetical lectures drew great crowds, and Carl Olof Rosenius (1816–68), who stressed a theology of "objective justification" which he personalized by an emphasis on Bible study and soul-searching. Scandinavian immigrants to America in the nineteenth century brought this intensely pietistic spirituality with them.[20]

Pietism in America blossomed. The stark necessities of human survival on the frontier called for theological adjustments, a declining emphasis on sacramental, liturgical form, and an increased emphasis on personal visitation and witnessing. Pietists founded schools and hospitals, orphanages, and homes for unwed mothers. They opposed slavery, worked for prison reform, criticized the abuses of wealth and power, advocated the rights of women and children, and fought for the abandonment of war.

"Above all," writes Olson, pietists "provided for the frontier Christian a sense of identity, that the faithful remnant community could be an island of love in the midst of the wilderness."[21]

Westerhoff and Holmes locate St. Benedict and Charles Wesley within this genus of spirituality.

When the K/H tendency becomes excessive, we have the "heresy of pietism," with its tendency toward emotionalism and excessive concern for feelings and right experience.

Though there are notable exceptions, I think you'll find the preponderance of television evangelists to be of this type. Clearly there's a good market for this brand of spirituality today. At times it gets exaggerated into a theology of glory that knows only of victory and success. Moral convictions are propagated emphatically. Salvation is assured triumphantly, in ways that appear to me to compromise the cross.

Lyle E. Schaller, a respected consultant and commentator on the American church scene, in an article he aptly entitled "The Unraveling of Tradition," gave four reasons why mainline churches are slipping while their nondenominational counterparts are taking off. The reasons have to do with four characteristics that one finds in the emerging development of our society's religious subculture. There also may be clues here helping to explain some of the recent migration from K/M to K/H spirituality.

1. Personal religious experiences, rather than the promises of God, constitute the central validation of one's faith.

2. The centrality of word and sacrament has been supplemented by word and especially music.

3. A theology of glory overshadows the theology of the cross.

4. A far greater emphasis is placed on the immanence of God rather than the transcendence of God.[22]

One can see how this development reveals a compatibility with the large number of religious folk in America who would style their spirituality as K/H.

One other characteristic of this growing subculture is that the churches are typically built around the attractiveness of a magnetic preacher who possesses a strong personality and who appears committed to a long pastorate.

But enough of these left-brain approaches to this quadrant of spirituality. Let's take a more right-brain slant by way of some illustrative stories.

I begin with a dialog between a recent convert and an unbelieving friend:

"So you've been converted to Christ?"
"Yes."
"Then you must know a great deal about him. Tell me: what country was he born in?"
"I don't know."
"What was his age when he died?"
"I don't know."

"You certainly know very little for a man who claims to be converted to Christ."

"You are right. I am ashamed at how little I know about him. But this much I do know: Three years ago I was a drunkard. I was in debt. My family was falling to pieces. My wife and children would dread my return home each evening. But now I have given up drink; we are out of debt; ours is now a happy home. All this Christ has done for me. This much I know of him!"[23]

To really know is to be transformed by what one knows. This is the stuff of spirituality for a K/H.

And here follows a story to illustrate an unsavory potential to K/H piety, the development of an unhealthy scrupulosity resulting in pietism rather than piety.

Two Buddhist monks, on their way to the monastery, found an exceedingly beautiful woman at the riverbank. Like them, she wished to cross the river, but the water was too high. So one of the monks lifted her onto his back and carried her across.

His fellow monk was thoroughly scandalized. For two hours he berated him on his negligence in keeping the rule: Had he forgotten he was a monk? How did he dare touch a woman? And worse, carry her across the river? What would people say? Had he not brought their holy religion into disrepute? And so on.

The offending monk patiently listened to the never-ending sermon. Finally he broke in with "Brother, I dropped that woman at the river. Are you still carrying her?"[24]

Each time I chew on the sins of others, I suspect the chewing gives me more pleasure than the sinning gives the sinner.

Apophatic/Mind Spirituality (A/M)

Move with me next, and finally, to the Apophatic/Mind (A/M) quadrant in the upper left. In the samples with which I have worked, this has been the least populated of the four quadrants. The volition is dominant. A contemplative mysticism fuels a bold striving to proclaim God's kingdom and witness to it as a coming event.

Olson uses the formulation "The Spirituality of Social Action." I prefer "The Spirituality of Societal Regeneration" to distinguish it from the social action done by many K/H types. Not all A/M types will be adequately described by the following. I regard the Spirituality of Societal Regeneration as but a major subtype of the A/M quadrant.

The roots of this brand of spirituality are nourished by sources foundational to Western Christendom. Stirred by biblical cries of outrage in the face of injustices and sufferings of humanity—particularly the poor and powerless—and emboldened by the authority and power of the gospel, societal regeneratists are ready to tackle every force that stands in the way of peace, justice, and human rights.

It's like a John Calvin's advancing a spirituality that has little to do with a lonely pious individual's striving to become more like Christ and much to do with a church and state being restyled in ethically telling ways to reflect their belonging to Christ.

The civil rights leadership of a Martin Luther King Jr., the political activism of a Dag Hammerskjold, the Catholic socialism of a Dorothy Day, and the witness of an Albert Schweitzer in his African hospital all partake of this brand of spirituality to at least some degree, as do components of liberation theology and proponents of Sojourners magazine.

This is the type of spirituality that provides the modern martyr— the civil disobedience type. This spirituality involves an intense and urgent sense of conflict and stress. Indeed, conflict and stress become the marks of the effective and faithful witnessing-worker in the world. There will be no peace until wars cease, no rest until justice is established. Hence, high burnout!

God provides the sustaining resources, often through small-group worship life, such as is practiced by the Sojourners staff, and by reaching out connectionally to others in a network of mutual support.

Persons with these spiritual commitments are not isolated within any confessional or denominational heritage. Theological perspectives frequently are not readily apparent. While the pietist's kind of social activism generally targets the immoral person, the social regeneratist takes on systems of power that perpetuate injustice and inequity within the society. While the pietist may be content to witness for Christ in a darkened world out of love for Jesus and the

lost, the social regeneratist dares to confront the power bases of
evil in the name of the Coming One whose world this is. The
Christology that informs a spirituality of societal regeneration is
distinctly eschatological, if not apocalyptic.

In characteristic apophatic ways, the societal regeneratist "sees"
what cannot be seen—that this world has a cosmic destiny in its
belongingness to Christ. Until others see what they already know,
they choose to be about the spiritual task of challenging all forces
that victimize those whom Christ has claimed, demonstrating in
their own small way the peaceable dominion that is coming.

Sometimes one becomes a prophet in this tradition through the
door of protest. Amos protested: "I am no prophet, nor a prophet's
son; but I am a herdsman, and a dresser of sycamore trees, and the
Lord took me from following the flock, and the Lord said to me,
'Go, prophesy to my people Israel' " (Amos 7:14-15). Poor Amos!
Like Jeremiah and Jonah, he did not want to be involved as a
societal regeneratist, but the living encounter with his Lord drove
him on, and under its influence he thundered against the rich:
"Hear this, you who trample upon the needy, and bring the poor
of the land to an end . . ." (Amos 8:4).

In the midst of solitude, then, a person may receive a prophetic
vocation like that of an Amos. And he or she may struggle against
it. But the struggle will be in vain, and that person will be pursued
by the anointing words: "To all to whom I send you you shall go,
and whatever I command you you shall speak. Be not afraid of
them, for I am with you to deliver you, says the Lord" (Jeremiah
1:7-8).

Such anointed ones go into action and their action often is fruitful
because the Lord is with them. What frequently distinguishes their
work is the way in which they see problems—at their root and in
their totality.

The enlightened societal regeneratist no longer relies on "little
ego," but on a power that is greater. Such a one knows the wisdom
of John 15:5, where Jesus is reported saying: "Apart from me you
can do nothing." The apostle Paul gave it positive phrasing: "I can
do all things in him who strengthens me" (Phil. 4:13). On an
occasion when Paul got carried away to boast that he had labored
more than all the others, he was quick to correct himself: "It was

not I, but the grace of God which is with me" (1 Cor. 15:10). Little wonder that someone with that conviction gets things done that matter societally.

At its best, this spirituality of societal regeneration reveals itself stereophonically: emphatically insisting from the one side—we hold out for an apocalyptic dominion that can never find adequate political implementation in any institutions or governments of this world, while battling incessantly from the other side—we can and must increase the level of justice in all human institutions while not expecting to transform any of them into the Dominion of God.

Excessive spirituality of the A/M sort can turn into the heresy of moralism—exaggerated concern for right actions and condemnatory judgment on culture.

I have adapted an image provided by Joseph Sittler to show how an A/M mentality might react when encountering a piety that has turned soggy.

"To each his own," we like to say,
    thinking we demonstrate thereby our open-mindedness,
    broad tolerances, and piety about piety.
But face it.
Some piety is downright soggy.

The speaker combined facts with commitment.
There was substance and passion
    The subject was world hunger.

One response out of a soggy piety:
    "I hear what you say; it is very serious and we must do something about it. But I really trust the Lord. The world and they who are in it belong to him. He will see to it that. . . ."

"Next time," said Sittler, "I'll just throw a baseball at a feather pillow. Less effort for the same 'absorbed by sogginess' result."[25]

To dramatize the thoughtful vitality in this spirituality of societal regeneration, I have written the following statement in the "voice" of someone committed to doing something about poverty and powerlessness:

Throughout history, the rich have had a difficult time seeing that their prosperity is based on other people's poverty. We don't seem to understand that we have much more than we *need* because the poor have much less than they need. In the present international economic order, coffee, sugar, pineapples, tobacco, and bananas for rich people are a higher priority than bread and rice for the poor.

The question to be asked is not what we should *give* to the poor but when will we stop *taking* from the poor. The poor are not our problem; we are their problem. We give the poor and racial minorities what we don't want, then change our minds and take it back when it becomes desirable again. It makes no difference whether we call it urban development, "gentrification," or the "back-to-the-city movement," the poor get displaced.

We are told that the plight of the urban poor is steadily worsening. Are more massive outbreaks of urban violence required for America to care for its poor? That's a frightful commentary on our spirituality.

The Old Testament sees poverty as neither accidental nor natural, but rooted in injustice.

The idea that poverty is simply due to the failures of the poor; the idea that we are comparatively well off because of hard work, responsible risk-taking, and dutiful management; the idea that there is enough for everyone to live at *our* standard of living—all these are cruel myths that prevent us from seeing what the issue of poverty and powerlessness is about.

Jesus said. "No one can serve two masters; for either he will hate the one and love the other, or he will be devoted to the one and despise the other. You cannot serve God and mammon" (Matt. 6:24). Jesus is not giving advice with these words. He is not saying: "You ought not try to serve both God and money." He is not saying: "It's not a good idea; I'd rather you didn't." Jesus is saying that you *cannot* do it. It will not work. You cannot serve the two masters at the same time because they make rival claims on your time, your energy, and your resources.

As Christian witnesses in the church, we claim to share what is everlasting. Why then should it be so confounded hard for us to share things that do not last? Seventy million people are now on the edge of starvation. Four hundred million suffer from chronic malnutrition. In all, one billion people are not getting enough to eat. In a world where most people are poor and too many are hungry, a rich church is living testimony of idol worship. Our way of life is a violation of the God who in Jesus became poor.

There is forgiveness, to be sure. But there is also truth: any spirituality that doesn't result in a new economy among the believers is incomplete, if not unauthentic.

At a recent workshop, I was asked to recommend journals that I consider to be speaking out of each of the four quadrants. Here's what I said: A primary magazine source for A/H spirituality is *Spiritual Life*; for K/M, *The Christian Century*; for K/H, *Discipleship*; and for A/M, *Sojourners*. You may have more fitting samples to suggest. Why not balance your reading so that you regularly sample literary influences from all four types of spirituality?

At another workshop participants suggested that the Essenes might have belonged to A/H; the Sadducees to K/M; the Pharisees to K/H; and the Zealots to A/M. What do you think?

3 | Two Views of Spirituality

Today's Christians seem to believe God has not one but two plans of salvation, two paths to heaven, two models of spirituality. I'll call them Plan A and Plan B.

Plan "A" Spirituality

In Plan A, we work our way to God—a mentality pointed up by Gal. 3:10: "Those who depend on obeying the Law live under a curse. For the Scripture says, 'Whoever does not always obey everything that is written in the book of the Law is under the curse!' " (Today's English Version).

Note especially those three words in the middle of the verse: *Always obey everything*. To work our way to God, we need to know what it takes to get there. If we want Plan A—if we choose to do good to get to God—God says we must *always obey everything*. Let's take that apart, word by word.

Always means "all the time; invariably." It's not good enough to be obedient to God's will 50 percent of the time, or 80 percent, or 90 percent, or even 99.9 percent. If we slip but once, we fail, for Plan A demands we must *always* obey everything.

Day after day Adam and Eve walked in perfect obedience with God, enjoying the harmony of a close relationship. But just once, during one little five-minute interval, they disobeyed. The problem, you see, wasn't with the apple in the tree but the pair *under* the tree! Adam and Eve failed *always* to obey and were driven from the garden. How narrow of God! You and I with our generally tolerant inclinations are apt to say in relation to obedience that "*usually* is good enough." But Plan A says obeying is required *always*.

Always *obey* everything. Obey! Do you obey God's law to love others as yourself? "Well, I try," you say. But what good is it to "try" if God's Plan A requirement is to *obey*? You have to do it, not simply try to do it.

Suppose you committed a crime and were brought before a judge. Do you think the judge would let you go if you told him, "But, your honor, I tried not to." Under Plan A, God isn't going to grant us heaven simply because we tried to be good. Did we do it? Were we perfectly obedient?

Always obey *everything*. Perhaps you say, "Well, I've never embezzled money. I've never murdered anyone. I've never committed adultery. Why, there are lots of things I've never done. I've really got a pretty good record, all things considered, when it comes to obeying God's moral commands."

St. Paul, being well-trained in rabbinic law, knew well the almost countless commands in the Scriptures. Certainly as a conscientious Pharisee, he would have scored well on anyone's moral checklist, but yet he called himself a "lawbreaker." Paul knew well that if he missed in but one place, he was a lawbreaker.

Suppose you kept every law in the country except that you, on one occasion, accidentally killed a person. You kept all the other laws, but still you are a lawbreaker and could be put into prison. You have not conformed to Plan A, which requires that we obey everything God commands—*obey all*, not just those we choose or happen to keep.

An example of a man who came to Jesus with a Plan A mindset is seen in Mark 10:17-22: "As [Jesus] was setting out on his journey, a man ran up and knelt before him, and asked him, 'Good Teacher, what must I do to inherit eternal life?' " His question clearly implies that he thought he could *do* something to earn his way to heaven.

Jesus responded "You know the commandments: 'Do not kill, Do not commit adultery, Do not steal, Do not bear false witness, Do not defraud, Honor your father and mother' " (v. 19).

"Teacher," the man declared, probably interrupting, "all these I have observed from my youth." The response he made could well have been more than idle boast, for he was a pious man.

But Jesus, loving him, sad that he had one more thing to lay on him—the first and Great Commandment that he love the Lord with all his heart, soul, mind, and strength. But Jesus didn't put it that way because he knew the man wouldn't understand such terms, so he spoke in terms he would understand—in terms of money and security. Jesus knew the man to be an idolater with money, so he said: "Go, sell what you have, and give to the poor, and you will have treasure in heaven" (Mark 10:21).

The man had come to Jesus asking what he must do to receive eternal life. Jesus went down the traditional moral list. The man said he had done all those things, so Jesus simply went further until he came to something the man could not or would not do. The man clearly intended to come to God under Plan A, so Jesus applied Plan A vigorously: *Always obey everything.* And the man turned away sorrowfully. Evidently, he had interpreted God's command to always obey everything as "usually try most things."

Consider this example from Luke 10:25-28: "A lawyer stood up to put [Jesus] to the test, saying, 'Teacher, what shall I do to inherit eternal life?' He said to him, 'What is written in the law? How do you read?' And he answered, 'You shall love the Lord your God with all your heart, and with all your soul, and with all your strength, and with all your mind; and your neighbor as yourself.' " The lawyer probably rattled it off rapidly, for he knew it well and wanted Jesus to know that he knew it well.

"Right, do that and you're in," Jesus said in effect.

But that left the man with a problem. How was he to do those things? Who has done those things perfectly? Still, not willing to lose out, he tried to get by on a legal technicality. Clearly, he had his own special definition for "neighbor"—namely, all the people he liked and who in turn liked him. In short, that man's neighbors were limited to other good Jews.

After that, Jesus followed with the memorable parable of the good Samaritan (Luke 10:29-37). The hero of the story was a Samaritan, one of a people hated by the Jews. Jesus thereby brought the man to acknowledge by his own final redefinition of "neighbor" that he was not really following Plan A all the way.

We find Plan A illustrated time and time again in the Bible.

Always obey everything! How many of us can say we always obey everything? How many love God above all things? How many love their neighbors as themselves, keeping in mind Jesus' definition of a neighbor?

No other person except Jesus has ever kept or even come close to keeping all of God's commandments.

In one sense, Plan A is like the distance between San Francisco and Honolulu as viewed by a swimmer. Perhaps a champion swimmer could get 25 or more miles along the way. I would consider 500 yards a good effort. There's a great difference between 25 miles and 500 yards, but they both fall far short of reaching Honolulu.

To be sure, there's a tremendous moral difference between a sincere Christian who makes enormous effort to keep all of God's commandments and someone who seems to have no conscience whatsoever. Of course there's a significant moral difference between a citizen, who, for example, contributed $500 to the United Way and another who turns a deaf ear to all appeals for aid. But both are still infinitely short of always obeying everything.

And so, clearly, even as St. Paul says, those who attempt to come to God under Plan A—those who depend on obeying the law — live under a curse. "For the Scripture says: 'Whoever does not always obey everything that is written in the book of the Law is under the curse!' "

People who think they will get to God only because they are good, obedient Christians are under a curse. It's great to be a morally upright person, but that's no basis for making it under Plan A. If you believe you will get to God because you go to church, read your Bible, pray regularly, care about your neighbors, haven't imbibed in many worldly sins, and are even willing to attend an adult education class on Sunday morning—if you think those good marks are going to qualify you to live with God, you're under a curse. This isn't my theory. The Bible says it. Cursed is everyone who tries to make it to God under Plan A. You'll never make it to God under Plan A.[1]

Still, there are many who have tried it or who are trying it. Luther tried it for years. He was a model monk. For quite a while, he lived an awesomely austere life, cloistered away from the evils of the world, incessantly in prayer, subjugating his body and mind to the things of God. If ever monkery could make it to God, Luther would have. But he found no peace. There were always sins to confess. Something deep within him told him that no matter how hard he tried, he didn't obey everything, and so he was under a curse—a curse which drove him to near despair. But then Luther rediscovered by his study of Romans that God in his love has provided a Plan B—sort of a God-ordained spiritual welfare program.

Plan "B" Spirituality

In Romans 4:3-5, Paul begins by quoting Genesis: "For what does the scripture say? 'Abraham believed God, and it was reckoned to him as righteousness.' Now to one who works, his wages are not reckoned as a gift but as his due. And to one who does not work but trusts him who justifies the ungodly, his faith is reckoned as righteousness."

There is no work—no amount of goodness that you or I can do—to get God to accept us. Rather, I need to heed the invitation to a new relationship with God through Christ, or, in the words of this text, simply to put my faith in God who, for the sake of Christ, declares the guilty to be innocent.

Plan A tells us to always obey everything. But Plan B says to put our faith in the perfectly obedient Jesus.

One way to understand Plan B is to say that God fills the gaps where you and I fall short in not always obeying everything, and he loads the punishment on Jesus. Jesus gets our sins. And in return for them, you get credit for all the good that he did. In that great transaction on the cross, God took our sins and laid them on Jesus and took Jesus' earned righteousness and ascribed it to you. That's the fantastic Plan B!

See how it is illustrated in Acts 16:11-40. Paul had come to Philippi. He was welcomed into town by promptly being thrown into prison. About midnight Paul and Silas were praying and singing hymns to God. A violent earthquake hit, breaking the doors down and rattling the chains off. The gruff jailer, you can be sure, was normally no coward. Yet here he was, literally frightened almost to death. The jailer feared for his life, but he sensed that Paul and Silas possessed a special power of God. He came to them and asked a question we've heard many times before: "Men, what must I do to be saved?"

And now notice, Paul and Silas didn't say: "Read your Bible and don't forget to pray," though that's important. They didn't say, "Go to church and communion regularly, contribute liberally, and witness openly," though it's important to do that. No, they gave a simple Plan B answer: "Believe in the Lord Jesus," they said, "and you will be saved, you and your household" (v. 31).

In the Old Testament we find Plan B exemplified as well. Why was Abraham called a "man of God"? Was he such a paragon of virtue and righteousness that he merited God's favor? The following story from Gen. 12:10—13:1 might freshen your memory a bit.

When there was a famine in Palestine, Abraham and Sarai headed for Egypt where food was abundant. Now Sarai was a beautiful woman and Abraham, fearing for his life, said to Sarai: "Since you are so beautiful, when the Egyptians see you they will want you for themselves, and if they know that I am your husband they will kill me in order to get you. Therefore tell them you are my sister that it may go well with me because of you, and that my life may be spared on your account" (Gen. 12:13, paraphrased). Did God choose Abraham because he was truthful, honest, brave, and dependable? On the contrary, the record shows that Abraham lied to save his life. To save his own skin, he was willing to sell his wife Sarai into Pharaoh's harem. No, Abraham was hardly a giant in moral matters. Gen. 15:6 puts it quite simply: "And [Abraham] believed the Lord; and [God] reckoned it to him as righteousness." That's what he did: He trusted in the Lord, and that trust was counted to him as adequate for his salvation.

I'm wondering, dear reader, whether you know you are under Plan B. I'm wondering whether, for your salvation, you are holding to Christ alone? Or are you holding to Christ plus being good, being generous, being moral, being a respectable citizen, and being a faithful church member? Whenever you say or imply "Christ plus . . ." you are immediately sticking yourself back under Plan A, which condemns. For example, if you say I hold to Christ *plus* care for my family, you must ask, How much caring for family is enough? You see, as soon as you add the plus requirement, you're right back under Plan A. You set a standard you cannot and will not keep perfectly.[2]

But you say, "I've got to have faith in Jesus. How much faith will do?" Why do you suppose the Bible speaks of faith the size of a mustard seed? That parable assures us that the weakest, most childlike faith is sufficient. If it's holding to Christ alone, a little, weak, struggling faith will do. Such faith puts me under Plan B. God accepts me on the basis of that faith—a faith which God inspires and gives through the work of the Holy Spirit, as but one more example of God's all-sufficient grace.

Are we ready now to define *grace* as the undeserved love and favor of God for us? Grace is getting what I don't deserve. Mercy is not getting what I do deserve.[3]

Gift, mercy, and grace are words that sound so strange to the modern ear. Most of our experiences lie in the areas of merit, reward, and achievement. In a competitive world, those who make the best efforts normally achieve the best rewards. A businessperson put it this way: "No person can be successful working just a 40-hour week—not unless he or she is absolutely brilliant, and most people are not brilliant. It's like the old saying, 'The harder I work, the luckier I get.' "

That sort of thinking bombards our lives, doesn't it? It shapes us to the core of our being. So I'm not too surprised when confirmation students tell me, as they have on occasion, that they hope to get to heaven because they are trying hard to live a Christian life. That's Plan A thinking all the way.

I'm a great deal more distressed when I hear people who are lifelong church members speak about the moral life they've lived, the Golden Rule philosophy they've tried to follow. They imply, you see, that they've given Plan A a good ride and, at worst, they may need a little of God's grace to make up the difference somehow. But they think they don't need all that much grace because God knows they've tried hard enough. That kind of talk grieves me because it's straight out of a Plan A mentality and, upon the authority of the Bible, I say such a person is living under the curse of an uncertain eternal future. God says: Trust me alone; anchor your faith solely in Christ. In matters spiritual, leave slogans such as "trying harder" to car rental agencies.[4]

We're talking about what I see to be America's foremost spiritual dilemma: how to keep a grace-oriented religion alive in a capitalistic, earn-what-you-get environment. There's a major spiritual hazard that goes with generalizing a capitalistic merit mentality into all areas of life. Self-reliant, do-it-yourselfism may be okay for economics, but it makes for oppressive religion, and it's heretical Christianity.

Really, there are only two kinds of religion in the world. One is a religion of *mercy* and the other is a religion of *merit*. Those who hold to merit rely on personal effort and achievement. They think they can somehow buy, earn, or finagle their way into the dominion of God. Those who hold to mercy stand on God's unmerited grace and favor. Christians profess that God in Jesus Christ gives salvation as a free gift.

Before proceeding further, I want to share briefly from my own life how I came to know a Plan B spirituality.

My father was a pastor, so I was raised in a parsonage in central Texas. My live-in grandfather also was a pastor. My father often told me about my great-grandfather, among the very first Lutheran missionaries to come to Texas from Germany in 1850. My only living brother is a pastor and my only sister is married to a pastor. I have an uncle and a nephew who are pastors, as well as two cousins who are on the Lutheran clergy roster. A tobacco-chewing cousin, not one of the pastors, said at a Sager family reunion once that he was afraid to spit for fear of hitting a preacher downwind.

Don't you suppose in such a preacher-saturated family and church setting I would have grown up knowing all about grace? I lived in a Christian home tended by well-trained parents and grandparents. I had a long string of perfect-attendance Sunday school pins. I spent many summers of up to five weeks at vacation church school. I earned a bachelor's degree from a church college that required several courses in Christianity. I had plenty of opportunity to learn of grace. And, of course, the right words were said and the doctrinally correct formulas were spoken. Why, I could sing "Jesus loves me, this I know for the Bible tells me so" almost before I learned how to talk.

One of my earliest prayers, learned in German, went this way, in part: *"Hab' ich Unrecht heut' getan, sieh es, lieber Gott, nicht an. Deine Gnad' und Christi Blut machen allen Schaden gut."* Loosely translated, that means: "If today I have sinned, dear God, do not regard it. Your grace and Christ's blood make amends for all wrongs." That was a fairly grace-oriented prayer for a four-year-old to be saying, don't you think?

Yet somehow, amid so many grace-filled resources, another message was getting massaged into me. In Boy Scouts I was busy collecting merit badges. In school good efforts earned good grades, which won good commendations. While holding several small jobs, I discovered that dependable work paid off with periodic raises. In short, I was learning the Western frontier mentality of get-what-you-earn. I had to work hard to earn starting positions on the football and basketball teams. Coming out atop my classes for both my eighth grade and high school graduations won me the privilege to give valedictory addresses. My teachers and the principals told me, "You earned it."

A macho image of self-reliant do-it-yourselfism was getting fashioned and reinforced in all areas of my life. Hard work and dutiful thrift would ensure an economically sound future, I was taught. A good education would help assure professional success. The 12 Boy Scout laws would help me "be prepared" for anything life might dish out. What more does anyone need than to be trustworthy, loyal, helpful, friendly, courteous, kind, obedient, cheerful, thrifty, brave, clean, and reverent? And why should I not, by being good on top of all of that, win heaven as the super grand prize, the ultimate merit badge?

Oh, it didn't get taught that way. Instead, I was influenced by the unspoken conclusion fashioned in my psyche from all the systems and philosophies that shaped my thoughts and actions six-plus days a week. I say "six-plus" because I remember going to Luther League on Sundays and singing, "We are climbing Jacob's ladder."

It's not surprising then that I was a first-year student in seminary before I discovered that I'm not saved by my conduct—that's simply how I behave. Nor am I saved by my creed—that's simply what I believe. Nor am I saved by my church—that's simply where I belong.

I am saved by God's grace as I accept by faith God's gift of having redeemed me through Jesus, God's Son, my Savior.[5]

Salvation is more than claiming beliefs. James points out (2:19) that even the devils believe. Intellectual insight, even when accompanied by emotional response (the devils tremble while believing), does not save. Mere mental assent to even the grandest Christian teachings does not produce life eternal.

Salvation is more than behaving. The Bible is compellingly clear that it is not by conduct that we are saved. The Rich Young Ruler in Luke 18:18-30 behaved properly; one would be hard pressed to find a more decent chap. Yet Christ told him: "One thing you still lack" (v. 22). The Bible speaks plainly: Justifying merits do not come from our own efforts. Most every epistle of Paul thunders: "Not by works of righteousness that we have done."

Salvation is more than belonging. Church membership does not save. Judas Iscariot belonged to the right group. If any group ever qualified as the "authorized group," it certainly would have been "the Twelve." They were handpicked by Christ. Yet even a member of that select company was called a "son of perdition," lonely in his lostness.

God wants and expects us to believe, to behave, and to belong, but concern with these things as primary is like a lifeguard inquiring first about a drowning person's philosophy, correct street address, or skinned shin. The lifeguard's proper concern initially should be with the person's respiration. A drowning person's first and urgent need is for air! Life must be restored.

The indispensable starting point for the scriptural, Plan B model is God's initiation. Christians have an organic union with God through Christ, who said: "I am the vine, you are the branches. They who abide in me, and I in them, it is they that bear much fruit, for apart from me you can do nothing" (John 15:5).

Jesus knew that the Holy Spirit must come for his disciples to be effective in their mission. "But you shall receive power when the Holy Spirit has come upon you; and you shall be my witnesses in Jerusalem and in all Judea and Samaria and to the end of the earth" (Acts 1:8). The Holy Spirit delivers to us what God has given us in Jesus. As the Spirit makes Christ present in our lives, we become spiritual because it is no longer we who live, but Christ who lives in us. (Gal. 2:20).

The Holy Spirit is always the initiator in our spiritual life, because Christ's role is primary. That which is done "in Christ" is spiritual, no matter how ordinary it may appear. That which is done apart from Christ is done "in sin," no matter how pious or noble it may appear. Spiritual growth is growth *in Christ*.

Some practical questions that arise from these two views of spirituality are:

1. Can I keep the dominant philosophy that rules my work-a-day world from contaminating my understanding and experience of God's grace?[6]

2. Do I adequately acknowledge the Spirit's role in my spiritual life? At the end of the day, do I adequately acknowledge God's role in my journeying and give appropriate thanks?[7]

3. Do I see the goal of my spirituality to recognize and respond to the continual movements of the Spirit, for the Spirit always will lead me toward greater union with Christ and greater love and service of God and others?

Highlighting the Two Views in Relation to the Apostles' Creed

In First Article Perspective—On Creation

As viewed through Plan A:

If I . . .
    (a) obey the precepts of a creation spirituality;
    (b) prove to be a worthy steward of creation through . . . ; and
    (c) honor the Creator by . . . ;
then I . . .
    (a) shall be blessed in innumerable creative ways;
    (b) shall attain meritorious status as a faithful steward; and
    (c) shall receive both temporal and eternal rewards from the Creator God

As viewed through Plan B:

Because . . .
  (a) our creator God has created me and all that exists;
  (b) has given me and still preserves to me all that I need for life and meaning; and
  (c) has blessed me with an abundance beyond my deserving or needing;

therefore . . .
  (a) I shall thank God;
  (b) I shall praise God; and
  (c) I shall serve and obey God.

In Second Article Perspective—On Redemption

As viewed through Plan A:

If I . . .
  (a) love Jesus devotedly;
  (b) serve Jesus exemplarily; and
  (c) follow Jesus faithfully;

then I . . .
  (a) shall live in the love of Jesus;
  (b) shall serve my way into the dominion of God;
  (c) shall end up where Jesus is.

As viewed through Plan B:

Because our redeeming God . . .
  (a) has sent Jesus Christ, true God begotten of the Father and true man, born of the Virgin Mary, to be my Lord;
  (b) has redeemed me through the precious blood and innocent suffering and death of Jesus Christ; and
  (c) has raised the crucified Messiah as resurrected Lord and honored Him as ascended Christ;

therefore I . . .
  (a) shall live under Christ's lordship in the dominion of new life;
  (b) shall serve my Savior in love through a life of gratitude; and

(c) shall partake of the new life that is no longer subject to death.

In Third Article Perspective—On Sanctification

As viewed through Plan A:

If I . . .
- (a) open myself to receive God's Spirit;
- (b) strive mightily and persistently to grow in faith, hope, and love; and
- (c) join regularly and helpfully with fellow Christians for piety, study, and action;

then I . . .
- (a) shall receive abundant spiritual blessings;
- (b) shall see my faith, hope, and love blossom progressively; and
- (c) shall be more and more enriched through that Christian fellowship.

As viewed through Plan B:

Because our sanctifying God . . .
- (a) has called me to faith through the Gospel;
- (b) has gathered me into the fellowship of the redeemed where sanctifying graces abound; and
- (c) has enlightened me with all needed gifts;

therefore I . . .
- (a) shall hold to that Gospel that found and holds me;
- (b) shall gather regularly with that family of God into which I was first gathered; and
- (c) shall share and show forth the enlightenings that I have received in the knowledge that I have been blessed to be a blessing.

4 | What Is Truly Spiritual?

When you are plunged under the waters of baptism," the Bible in effect says, "you not only get washed, you die!"

Now isn't that language a little strong? Don't we prefer thinking of baptism as a quietly joyous, peaceful event? Oh, on occasion, a baby may voice a whimpering protest, but generally it's such a pleasant, smiling event that we are tempted to ignore the more violent, wrenching dimensions of what's going on.

Paul says in Romans 6:4: "We were buried therefore with him by baptism into death. . . ."

At times I regret that Lutherans have settled for baptism by sprinkling or pouring. For the most part, we who baptize mostly infants are afraid even to get the frilly dress wet. I wonder how our theology of baptism might expand if we pushed babes down three times completely under the water until they burst out gasping, as if seeking to escape from God's washing. That rite might better fit our talk of baptism as the bath that drowns, although parents and relatives of a baptized child would probably call the police or an ambulance or both!

To be overwhelmed by those divine waters is to die to our old false securities. It's to know there is no life except that which comes to us from beyond us. The life that comes is the rising to a new life in Christ. And that can happen only on the other side of a dying to self.

Baptism is a divine reclamation project: a going under and a coming out, a death and a resurrection, a dying and a rising, a dress rehearsal for death as well as a trial run for resurrection. It is living hereafter as one who belongs to that One who has marked me forever with the sign of the cross. It's not a mark that washes off, but one that has been washed in—soaked into me through and through.

The calves I used to help hold for branding when I was growing up in Texas kicked when the red-hot branding iron seared the mark that announced where they belonged.

Personally, I'm inwardly delighted just a little when a child at baptism kicks up a fuss. It simply reminds me that the fire of the Spirit is involved in a branding operation for which a few kicks are quite appropriate.

Let the mixed images stand. I assure you, I kick around repeatedly as the baptismal drama gets reenacted in my daily life through the repeated drowning of the old Adam whom I have found to be a better swimmer than that old cat with its proverbial nine lives.

I'm talking about a Plan B life-style. I'm saying that Plan B living is impossible until we've died to self, until we've given up control, until we've submitted to that One who has marked us in our baptism as belonging eternally to the triune God.

By implication, I've been saying that God is committed to one major Plan B objective in the lives of all who know themselves to be Plan B people of God.

Maybe you've never stopped to consider that God is committed to one major objective in the lives of all people committed to a Plan B life-style.

What is the one major objective that God is committed to in the lives of all people committed to a Plan B life-style? *To conform us to the image of God's son.* It sounds biblical enough, but it comes off as mystifyingly theological—as something that could get us neck deep in tricky theological waters.

Jesus provides the simple answer to our question about the nature of the image of God's son into which God would conform us: "For the Son of man also came not to be served but to serve, and to give his life as a ransom for many" (Mark. 10:45).

There it is. No mumbo jumbo. Just a straight-from-the-shoulder declaration: Jesus came to serve and to give. And God desires the same for us and from us. God is in the business of fashioning servants, not celebrities.

When Jesus gathered his disciples for the Last Supper, they were having trouble, as you recall, determining who was the greatest among them. It was no new issue. It simply hadn't been raised in quite this guise before.

Well, what was the issue? Whenever there is a question about who is the greatest, usually the deeper underlying issue is, instead, who is the least. Isn't that generally the crux of the matter for us? Most of us know we will never be the greatest, but we're determined not to be the least.

Gathered at the Passover feast, the disciples were keenly aware that someone needed to wash everyone else's feet. The problem was that the only people who washed feet were the least, not the greatest. So their feet remained caked with dirt because no one wanted to be considered the least—until Jesus took a towel and a basin and redefined greatness.

And as Jesus lived out servanthood before them with a towel on his arm, he called them to a Plan B life-style. "If I then, your Lord and Teacher, have washed your feet, you also ought to wash one another's feet. For I have given you an example, that you also should do as I have done to you" (John 13:14-15).

In some ways it might be preferable to hear Jesus' call to deny father and mother, houses and land, for the sake of the gospel, than to hear these words about washing feet. Radical self-denial at least has about it the feel of noble adventure. But to be banished to the mundane, the ordinary, the seemingly trivial as though we were nothing more than a slave is a bit much to swallow. Indeed, when ego puffs up, that pill simply won't go down. That's why the me-in-control self must die before conformity to the Son is possible.

You know, in a sense, the whole world is like that Upper Room filled with proud hearts and dirty feet where disciples were willing to fight for a throne but not for a towel. Things haven't changed a lot since then.

A story is told of a young boy who often got into mischief in his Sunday school class. Often the teacher tried to advise and correct him. One day the boy had been particularly disruptive and the teacher had to interrupt class to chide him. The boy, realizing that he was once again the cause of trouble, looked up at his teacher and with surprising insight and thoughtfulness said: "I know I cause you and my classmates lots of problems. You always seem to do the right thing, and I always seem to do dumb, wrong things. If you could just crawl down inside of me and stay there, then maybe I could do good things, too."

Have you ever looked up into the face of your heavenly Father and said in near desperation: "Lord, I messed up again. You are infinitely good and you always do the right thing. I seem to be an expert in lousing up situations. Often I do the wrong thing, or maybe I do the right thing but at the wrong time or in the wrong way. If you would just get down inside of me and stay there, then I, too, could live as both of us want."

And, of course, that's exactly what God wants to do. God wants to and can get down deep inside of us, through the Holy Spirit, and make us like Christ. God wants to take us over and make us over. In deep, where the surgeon can't get with the scalpel or the psychiatrist with her probing. There the Holy Spirit will dwell and work, purifying our desires and motives, helping us control our thoughts and emotions, directing our wills and ambitions.

Have you ever consciously surrendered yourself to the power of that purifying, directing Holy Spirit?

We who have been baptized into Christ are united to him through faith. Faith is the key. When we consciously place our trust in Christ, we surrender our lives to the Holy Spirit, who is Christ in us.

As marvelous a thing as baptism is, it is not magic. It is faith that receives baptism—and therefore the work of the Holy Spirit—into our lives.

I am frequently a house guest in someone else's home, and hosts characteristically go out of their way to make me feel welcome. Often they say something like, "Let's take just a minute to show you around first. Here's your bedroom. The bath is right down the hall. We've put out some fresh towels for you. You're welcome, of course, in the family room. If you want to read or watch TV, just make yourself at home. Let us know if there is anything you need."

Now what does all that mean? As I interpret what they say, it means that as a special courtesy during my short stay certain rooms and facilities in the house are being shared for my convenience. I don't interpret it to mean that I can walk anywhere in the house at will and help myself to anything that I might see, or that I might boss any of the various members of the household in accord to my desires. I'm in the house, but in the very limited role of a *guest*. When I get back to my own home, the situation is different. There I'm no longer a guest. I'm owner and master—if I can get away with it! At any rate, I am completely free to move around in the house. I claim ownership of the home and its furnishings in partnership with my family.

Christians are people who open the door of their hearts and allow the spirit of Christ to walk across the threshold of their lives. However, what many say, in effect, is this: "Lord, welcome. Let me show you to your room—the one with the big 'R' on the door. That's my religious corner. I thought you'd be most comfortable there. Most of the other areas of the house probably wouldn't interest you anyway. Furthermore, they're rather private. No admission without permission."

And so, though the Holy Spirit is present in the house by faith, the person is resisting the Spirit's desire to transform him or her in the image of Christ. And though the Spirit will take bold initiatives to knock on other doors, the Spirit is absolutely respectful of the owner's right to prevent entry.

What the Spirit desires is that we hand over a complete set of keys so that every closet, every drawer, and every file is open to inspection, cleaning out, and shaping up.

Where the Holy Spirit is in control, there will be holiness. As long as we do not block the Spirit's work in our lives, the Spirit will find and permeate every part of our being and keep on cleansing, empowering, and enlivening.

But every day we mar that relationship by self-will and disobedience. And this willfulness must be drowned again and again by daily repentance. How blessed we are that the grace of our Lord Jesus empowers even that repentance, for only those who know themselves to be loved unconditionally dare to be honest about who has been in control.

We are called to surrender to a loving, gracious Lord who desires nothing but the best for us. Certainly the God who made us should know what that might be. God wants to make something out of our lives for God's honor and glory and the blessing of others. If we consent to that, God assures we will be blessed beyond what we can imagine. It is true that we will not be able to have our way in everything—our way must die continually—but we will find that God's way always is the best way.

Today, our Lord is coming again to each one of us and saying:

"Daughter/Son, do you have that life I have given you?"

"Why yes, Lord, you know I'm still alive, and I do thank you for that."

"Well, I want you to give your life back to me."

"But Lord, I only have one life, and it's so short at that. Do you know what you are asking? Why must I give it back to you?"

"Because you are twice mine, I want you to give it back to me."

And here's the marvel of it. The moment we truly consent to give our lives back to God, God says to us: "I offer myself to all, but only those who surrender everything to me are open to receiving my all."

And with that, God fills us with all God's blessings, including peace, joy, love, and power. God also hands back the life that we have just surrendered, and it truly is a new creation—redeemed and transformed for God's glory.

You and I don't return to God on our own initiative. Repeatedly we are returned through the wooing and winning mediation of the Holy Spirit.

5 | A Spirituality for Our Times

The gospel is the central treasure of the church, the content of its preaching and teaching, the heartbeat of its witness through mission and service. A spirituality that is gospel-centered is a spirituality that is anchored in the *evangel* or good news of God's grace in Jesus Christ. This book is a response to the gospel, as is all gospel-centered spirituality. Because the gospel is a generative power of God, the response to it partakes of it. Hence, all pride in spirituality as "my response" is swept away by the pervasive giftedness of the entire process. As the apostle Paul puts it: "And we all, with unveiled face, beholding the glory of the Lord, are being changed into his likeness from one degree of glory to another; for this comes from the Lord who is the Spirit" (2 Cor. 3:18).

As a result of my study of spirituality, I have been impressed by the *variety and complexity* of what I have found. Clearly, one can discern no single pattern within the genius of so many spiritual masters. Baron von Hugel wrote, "Souls are never dittos." Nor does the context for spirituality, the historical interplay of cultural and religious situations, ever remain static. It follows then that we allow one another a spirituality unique to our own person and circumstance, yet within the wide circle of sensibility that the Church provides. One of the major benefits of this awareness is that we are saved from a narrow, shallow, or doctrinaire notion as to the nature of Christian spirituality.

Several metaphors wind their way through the literature of spirituality. The one I prefer is the *concept of journey*. Living is making the journey of the spirit. To avoid that journey is only to exist. The starting point for the spiritual journey is a gift. The Christian journey begins when, as repentant and forgiven people of God, we ever so tentatively risk letting our lives be shaped and empowered by Jesus Christ. Progress on the journey is fidelity to Jesus. Our spiritual journey then is not so much from God nor toward God, but *with* God. In finding Emmanuel ("God with us"), we discover ourselves to have been found. Being found by a God who remains hidden prompts us to fancy ourselves as seekers.

Two images, *the mountain* and *the desert*, stand out as characteristic of the terrain over which the journey leads us. Both entail risk. We must be willing to confront the demons in the desert[1] as well as be served by the angels on the mountain. There will be peak experiences as well as dark nights of the soul. The temptation remains to "make three booths" (Mark 9:5) as a way of holding onto spiritual highs. Or we may try to capture our experience of God in some propositional way. Of this we may be confident: no one has captured the ineffable God by precise verbal formulae or rigid spiritual disciplines.

Helen Kromer, in these lyrics from the musical "For Heaven's Sake," reminds us which way is "up" in evangelical spirituality.

> He was a flop at thirty-three!
> His whole career was one of failure and of loss;
> But the thing that's so distressful
> Is he could have been successful
> > But instead of climbing up,
> > He climbed a cross![2]

Our culture conditions us to believe that all we need for wholeness is simply something *more*. Acquire more information, master more technique, enact more "doing" and we will move ourselves into some higher level of wholeness. The whole process avoids the cross, seeking to bring "abundant life" out of earthly life. The resurrection "up" only follows crucifixion. The necessity of *dying to the old* parameters of our existence, the necessity of letting go of things that warp and misshape and distort who we are goes with God's reclamation project. Why do we not bear more fruit in our Christian walk? Because the wind of pride too often blows out the light. The cloud of self-love repeatedly blinds. "Metanoia" (turning from our willful ways) is refused again and again. In short, the fruit-bearing potential of the seed is lost because the seed has not first died.

When it comes to the techniques of spirituality, Augustine's word remains most fitting when he says: "We come to God by love and not by navigation." Or, to change the imagery, if we are slaves to a "cookbook" approach to spirituality, the Divine Chef may have difficulty exercising creativity within us. Anyone who insists on approaching God in some particular way will likely "get the way" rather than God. In other words, too much of what promises "training for the life of the Spirit" comes off as "straining for the life of the Spirit." I fancy that God smiles at all efforts to *wrench from God what is already given.*

I see better than before how the straightest road to transforming society may be the one that runs through profound mystical experience. The paradox of true mysticism is that *personal experience of God leads to social passion.* Love of God and love of neighbor are not two commandments, but one. American Christianity needs this deeper strain of spirituality, living contact with God as the source— not of world flight, but of the most intensely "practical" Christianity that has yet been known. "For everything there is a season" writes the preacher of Ecclesiastes (3:1). Why not seasons of contemplation followed by seasons of action followed by more seasons of contemplation?

We all need more Sabbath time. This is the best antidote I know for curbing our "hurry-worry sindrome." I suspect that those who honor the Sabbath will in time discover more deeply what Meister Eckhart meant when he said, "God is not found in the soul by adding anything but by a process of subtraction."

What if we understood spirituality primarily in terms of *fidelity to the ordinary demands of daily living*—that is, persevering through whatever radiance or grayness each day may bring? Getting carried away by heavenly things because we've given up on earthly ones is not the call of God. The aim of the Christian journey is not to have ecstatic experiences of God (although this might occur), nor personal fulfillment (although this might occur as well), but to share in Christ's incarnational ministry and mission to the world. So, of course, spirituality has to do with care for neighbor as well as self-care, with solitude as well as stress, with challenging both corporate excesses and personal gluttony, with tending the poor and the weak as well as tending to our marriages.

A living faith is not something we have to carry; it, in fact, carries us. Though we cannot accelerate the development of our faith, we are nonetheless called to *cultivate our spiritual life*. Cultivation is a process of nurture and education, exercise and celebration. If we are impatient with ourselves and want to force ourselves to change, usually no good will come from it. No growth ever results from violence. Spirituality is better seen as process than product, for a Christian's *being* is in *becoming*. We don't acquire spirituality as though we possessed it. With St. Paul, we press on. Evangelical "becoming" calls for continual repentance, a continual new start in a new direction. It is a new start from sin to righteousness, from slavery to freedom, from unfaith to trusting God's promises, and from past to future.

Spirituality is not complicated, but it is demanding. It requires that we have *open hands and waiting hearts*, but being open and waiting is *not* what I've been conditioned for. My hands tend to grasp, to get, to possess, to hold, and to keep. And my heart? Little wonder that one of the first works of the Spirit is to create a space in my bloated life for being open to God and to the gifts of God.

Two distortions are common as persons rather uncritically identify themselves with one or more spiritual leaders, gurus, or spiritual interest groups. One distortion happens as would-be spiritual guides emphasize strongly the disciplined character of spiritual journeying. Chances are good that in their company you will end up with an overdose of willpower. The ditch on the other side of the road belongs to those who speak in relaxed tones of the easily embraced essence of spirituality. Chances are good that with them you will inherit an overdose of sentimentality. A great need persists for competent evangelical guides who know themselves to be called and claimed by Christ, who are committed to a disciplined journey of faith, and who welcome fellow travelers on the way.

As I reflect on my spiritual journeying, these observations appear as valid:

• You won't be given "more than you can bear" in the strength of the Empowering One.

• You will be led by "a way you do not know," to become a channel for grace "in ways you cannot predict."

• And the best you can do is to offer continual gratitude, praise, and thanksgiving for the grace that has found you and will not let you go.

All this concern about spirituality could be hazardous to our spiritual health. The dangerous paradox here is that our spirituality, our morality, *our piety could become the last and strongest fortress of sin.* There we can retreat and practice our newfound works of spiritual development in defense against God's assault on our self-reliance and on our refusal to let God be God with us.

A renewed Christian spirituality will be concerned with the *recovery of the vision of God in the contemporary world.* It will seek to speak of God and of the deep things of the spirit in ways that are both faithful and meaningful—hence, joining mystery with clarity. Solely to take refuge in mystery may lead to a spirituality of escape, but undue preoccupation with what is clear may lead to distortion. Mystery requires clarity lest mystery evaporate; clarity requires mystery lest clarity be corrupted. A spirituality truly drawn from Word and sacraments unites the mystery and clarity inherent in God's graciousness. Humbly and carefully, it will also take account of the insights presented by the natural and social sciences, by depth psychology, by the secular quest for enriched consciousness, by Marxism, by eastern mysticism, and by other systems that claim to speak to or about the destinies of life. The probes will be fueled by the conviction that the risen Christ is Lord over all or no lord at all, but will resist an air of triumphalism.

It will be a spirituality that is rooted in the experience of God in the life of Jewish people, but it will *find its center in Jesus Christ,* seeing in the Christ the fullness of the Godhead dwelling bodily. It will see in Jesus both God incarnate and a human companion, the divine revealed and the human raised up. It will rejoice in the divine gifts of matter and of sexuality. It will be an incarnational, materialistic spirituality. It will take the stuff of life with utmost seriousness and declare both the need for and the promise of a cosmic redemption. As such, it will fight against that pervasive docetic tendency to underplay the humanity of Jesus as a model for true humanness.

It will be *a spirituality that is communal.* The Christian journey is fundamentally a communal experience, God having fashioned us as "the people of God." A growing life with God leads us more deeply into a sense of solidarity, not only with the whole Christian Church but with the whole human family of which we are a part. Yet, the spirituality for which I speak will insist on preserving the delicate balance between the individual and the community. Demands of togetherness dare not cancel out all requirements of privacy. The openness of community ought not demand searing self-revelation, with no holds barred. Respect for individuals honors God's gifts of particularity. At the same time, honoring the church as the one body of Christ and the whole human community as a creative gift respects God's way of doing business with humans.

It will be a spirituality *having a global consciousness.* Everything is, in actuality, connected. I'm astounded, for instance, by the information shared by biologist John Storer that every square mile of soil on our earth contains particles from every other square mile of soil on our earth. That's interconnectedness! Little wonder that scientist joins mystic in urging that we are all involved with one another and all part of one another. Our journey into spiritual freedom is inevitably a journey of discovering inter-relatedness. The notion of "privatism" must recede. Fear is the fruit of privatism. Fear blocks interchange. Perfect love casts out fear. Living connectedly is a product of loving hospitably.

It will be *a eucharistic spirituality.* At its heart will be the celebration of the Eucharist, the sacrament of Christ's body and blood. The Eucharist is not just a source of grace, but the acting presence of the risen Christ among us. We come to recognize Christ both in the Eucharist and in those who share Christ's nature. Individualism and subjectivism remain our favorite eucharistic heresies. Too many people still see the Eucharist as the union of individual souls with God alone and are more concerned with gaining grace than with strengthening their commitment to Christ's mission in the world, for which this meal nourishes us.

Moslem mystics called Sufis tell a story cautioning the one whose house is too small for elephants to think twice before becoming the best friend of an elephant trainer. You might find yourself sharing your habitat with the friends of your friend! Similarly, Jesus never comes alone as indwelling guest. He brings with him all those "least of them" who require elephantine graciousness.

It will be a spirituality that will take seriously the experience of God in *women's history* and the forgotten or neglected insights of writers who have experienced and described God in *feminine attributes* and ways. It will not disdain the long overdue and still-awkward business of moving toward a more inclusive language both in and out of the sanctuary.

It will be a spirituality that *affirms choice.* No history is written in advance, which is simply to say that human choice shapes history. Since our God has chosen self-revelation in and through history and has gifted us with freedom, we fashion history through choice. "Choose you this day whom you will serve"—the ancient words of freedom still call all to creative choice and shared responsibility. To relinquish choice is to relinquish freedom. Freedom and abundant life (what Christ came to provide) are twin descriptions of one reality.

It will be *a spirituality of justice and peace*, as much as of compassion and charity. To effect that balance of emphasis will require a major overhaul of ecclesiastical priorities. A spirituality for our time will seek to know and follow God in the struggle against racism, sexism, ageism, and all other forms of domination. It will involve itself at multiple levels and in multiple ways in the campaigns against poverty, world hunger, and inequality. It will not stop with binding up the wounds of the traveler on the Jericho road. It will insist as well that the constituted authorities help make the Jericho road safe for all travelers.

It will be a spirituality of pain, of negation, of darkness, of letting go, and of letting be. It will see in the passion and death of Jesus the heart of the gospel. It will *proclaim a theology of the cross* that announces not only the pardoning crucifixion of Jesus on our behalf, but that also calls us "in Christ" to be crucified with him, to give to death the old self that must die before we may rise with Christ to newness of life.

It will be a spirituality *holistic in scope.* God's invitation to new life touches and seeks to involve the totality of a person's life and person, not just a small "religious corner" or a slice of life called "the spiritual me." Even as the whole "me" was redeemed, so the whole "me" is on the journey into freedom, which is the upward call of God in Christ Jesus. How I spend my money is as much a matter of spirituality as is how I say my prayers. My exercise of citizenship, my sex life, and my attitude toward the neighbor's dog all are parts of the mix called my life in grace.

It will be a spirituality of water and of fire, of cleansing and of purifying, of *renewal and of spiritual warmth.* In that sense, it will be a charismatic spirituality.

It will be a spirituality *fit for children.* The world has become a dangerous place for children. When such elements as innocent joy, eager trust, and endless inquisitiveness are in danger of becoming extinct, it's time to awaken. If we want to grow spiritually, we should spend more time observing children and praying for childlike attributes.

It will be a new ecclesial spirituality that liberates the Christian from individualism on the one hand, and from an overemphasis on the legal authority of ecclesiastical institutions on the other. It will be *ecumenical without sacrificing grounding in a particular confession or spirituality.* The Greek root word *oikos* means "one house." What if we think of the "one house" as God's house, where we all are together in a mammoth-sized den? We're together with our plurality of spiritualities, but we are searching responsibly for corresponding unity amid assorted difference. The alternative is simply unacceptable— for if we baptize a radical pluralism and allow that to justify our return to tribal narrowness, we lose all sense of the common *ecumene.*

It will be a spirituality calling for *three parallel lines of development.* There is the line of our *growth in love,* the line of our *growth in poverty of spirit,* and the line of our *growth in prayer.* Love penetrates everything. Yet, since redeeming love is the love of Christ shared with me and given to me, it can come to me only insofar as I am open to God in poverty. Openness to God in poverty of spirit fosters a living personal relationship with a living God. The more we seek to cultivate that relationship, the more we pray. Prayer then is not simply a duty or an obligation, but a personal need for a faith come of age.

It will be *an eschatological spirituality countering the pseudo-eschatology of secularism*. It will be in continuity with the eschatological worldview of the early church in announcing that the ultimate horizon of the world, its true goal, is the dominion of God in which "God may be everything to everyone" (1 Cor. 15:28). Granted, this "good world created by God" has been stolen from God by sin and death and enslaved to the "prince of this world." But by the holy Spirit's work within us, we can see and experience that this world is the arena in which we have been called to new life, made part of a "new creation," and given a foretaste of the world to come, the dominion of God's own fashioning. Though our true life is now "hid with Christ in God" (Col. 3:3), our final destiny is not in doubt, being as sure as are the promises of God.

It will be a spirituality fostering holistic renewal—*personal, corporate, conceptual, structural, and missiological*. To be genuine, renewal must be personal and corporate, touching both individual lives and whole communities of believers. To be long-lasting, renewal must become conceptual and structural. God's Spirit may be hindered by wrong ideas as well as by cold hearts. We need new vision for the church's life and mission. We need effective structures lest renewal becomes a fond memory and not a new way of life. And finally, to be fully dynamic, renewal must reach the missiological level. The church, Emil Brunner reminds us, exists by mission as fire exists by burning.

It will be a spirituality *empowered by grace*. The notion that we can cleanse ourselves or give up our sinful attitudes and actions is pharisaical delusion. Our transformation is by grace alone. Grace transforms our hearts, resulting in an awakening to who we are in Christ and what he is about for us, in us, and through us.

Part Two | Our Spiritual Journey

Introduction

In Part One, I argued that spiritual life and growth are the work of God. Following the pattern of the New Testament (see, for example, the first three chapters of Ephesians), spirituality anchors in the indicative of God's saving activity in our behalf. Part Two is modeled on the last three chapters of Ephesians which begin with "I entreat you, then . . ." and outline attitudes and actions which befit the new life given in Christ.

The format of Part Two, a brief introductory narrative on themes central to spirituality coupled with an annotated bibliography, evolved from earlier full-length chapters and represents a concession to working within allotted space. The chief benefit of the redesign lies in providing reading and study cues for readers who may have specialized interests and who do not wish to invest equal energies in assorted topics. Also, the brief highlighting of sources seems compatible with the reading preferences of many modern folk.

All of the annotated sources are a valued part of my personal library. Readers may wish to order sources judged to be useful directly from the publisher or from a favorite bookseller. Libraries would be the depositories of sources no longer in print, and such titles have been noted for your convenience. Information about authors was current as of the time of a book's publication.

Dietrich Bonhoeffer, a theologian, pastor, and Christian martyr, called us to reclaim the New Testament and evangelical perspective on spiritual exercises. He wrote: "In all these exercises following confession, the aim is to preserve the grace that has been received and to live from it. They are an ongoing element in the Christian life. To those who find them repugnant they appear as a hard law. To those who are willing, however, they are a gentle yoke in which our wild cravings find a rest."[1]

6   Worship and the Eucharist

God is actively seeking worshipers. Jesus declared: "The true worshipers will worship the Father in spirit and truth, for such the Father seeks to worship him" (John 4:23).

Worship that sets us before God can transform us. To stand before the Holy One of eternity is to change. Is it too much to say that if worship does not change us, it has not been true worship?

A striking feature of worship in the Bible is how people gathered in what can best be called a "holy expectancy." How do we cultivate this holy expectancy? Or does it just happen when we see a sufficiently high and holy vision of our living God? When two or more come into public worship with a holy expectancy, it can change the atmosphere of the worship setting.

A little girl went into a cathedral during the week when it was empty. When she came out she was asked what she did while in there. She replied, "Oh, I just loved God a little."

A little boy said his ABC's for his prayer. He said that God could make the right words out of the letters.

Ask Christians to tell you what happened to them when they report having had "a good worship experience," and you'll get a host of answers:

• My perspective and energy for caring and coping have been renewed.

• I experienced a deep sense of peace and calm.

• I have been reincorporated with fellow worshipers into that body which keeps alive the Christian experience of God.

• My narrow vision and individualistic perspectives have been broadened and deepened.

• I have a freshened sense of identity as being a child of royal lineage, an heir of God's dominion, a daughter or son of the most high.

Service flows out of worship. Service as a substitute for worship is idolatry. Just as worship begins in holy expectancy, it ends in holy obedience. Holy obedience saves worship from becoming an opiate or an escape from the pressing needs of modern life. Worship enables us to hear the call to service clearly so that we respond, "Here am I! Send me" (Isa. 6:8).

The Eucharist

A stained-glass window in a Paris church depicts the winepress of God. OK. You might guess that the wine press is intended to squeeze out juice from the earth's sour grapes so wine may be made for the Eucharist. But this winepress is pressing down on Christ, and his blood seeps out from his veins into the waiting chalice.

Frederick Buechner invites us to think of the Eucharist as a spiritual square dance in which partners get exchanged. We go ostensibly to dance with God, but end up beside some unlikely partners. In fact, God says that if we're not willing to experience this exchange of partners, we're kidding ourselves if we thought we had been twirling around with God.

For Further Reading

Brand, Eugene L. *Baptism: A Pastoral Perspective*. Minneapolis: Augsburg, 1975. (Out of print.)

Eugene Brand, a longtime leader in worship renewal, sees Christian renewal for mission rooted in a revitalized appreciation of Holy Baptism. He blends biblical, historical, theological, liturgical, and pastoral perspectives in a study that remains readable as it informs. 127 pages.

Ditmanson, Harold H. *Grace: In Experience and Theology.* Minneapolis: Augsburg, 1977. (Out of print.)

Grace—a summarizing Christian word, the heart of the gospel, the unifying principle through which all Christian doctrines are interconnected, best observed in Jesus Christ. Grace, a datum of experience before it became a dogma of theology. A deeply mysterious surprise. God's hold on us. The ultimate context within which all created objects, persons, and events have their being. Grace creates and calls forth gratitude and Christian service. This book based on a lecture series is written with care and clarity by the late Harold Ditmanson, professor of religion at St. Olaf College, Northfield, Minnesota. 296 pages.

Jungkuntz, Richard. *The Gospel of Baptism.* St. Louis: Concordia, 1968. (Out of print.)

Jungkuntz is probably correct in his assertion that baptism appears to be of less significance in the church's parishes, in its popular literature, and in the lives of its members than preaching and the Eucharist. This book tries to tell how a Christian's baptism can be rich in meaning and power when one listens more closely to the witness of Holy Scripture. A former Lutheran pastor, seminary professor, and college provost, Jungkuntz sees in this sacrament of water and the Word power for life today. 137 pages.

Lehman, H. T., ed. *Meaning and Practice of the Lord's Supper.* Philadelphia: Muhlenberg Press, 1961. (Out of print.)

This book is intended for all who wrestle with the meaning of the Lord's Supper for the Christian community today. Five Lutheran scholars collaborate to trace the place the Lord's Supper has occupied in church history. This historical inquiry traces the variety of meanings attached to the Lord's Supper as well as the practices and malpractices associated with its use. Seven chapters with an index; 210 pages.

Marty, Martin E. *The Lord's Supper.* Philadelphia: Fortress Press, 1980.

This volume has 80 pages on the Lord's Supper by a Lutheran pastor, prominent religious leader, editor, lecturer, author, and Distinguished Professor of Divinity at the University of Chicago. You expect him to delve into the attitudes, beliefs, and practices that have grown up around this sacred ritual. What you might not expect is his engaging recreation of a day in the life of a contemporary believer who participates in the eucharistic service. Marty highlights the words "for you . . . for forgiveness" as the "commanding vision" in his exposition on the Lord's Supper.

Marty, Martin E. *The Word: People Participating in Preaching*. Philadelphia: Fortress Press, 1984. (Out of print.)

Can you recall five sermons you have heard through the years? Chances are that they were examples of "preaching with" rather than "preaching to." Following the sequence of participation involved in a typical order of worship, Marty discusses people's participation in receiving, sharing, and acting the Word. The kind of proclamation that best fosters spiritual growth is shared event. 112 pages.

Mulholland, M. Robert, Jr. *Shaped by the Word: The Power of Scripture in Spiritual Formation*. Nashville: The Upper Room, 1985.

Clearly one of the most important resources for spiritual formation is the Bible. According to Dr. Mulholland, Dean of the School of Theology at Asbury Theological Seminary, the way we approach Scripture determines how it will affect us. An informational approach may simply be another expression of our acquisitive nature and may keep us structurally closed to being addressed by God. A formational approach to Scripture recognizes that the Word of God addresses us in our brokenness, calls us to wholeness, and becomes the agent of transformation in that process whereby we are being conformed to the image of Christ. This book, which emerged from a lecture series, will be especially appreciated by those concerned with remaining spiritually Word-centered. 171 pages.

Pannenberg, Wolfhart. *Christian Spirituality*. Philadelphia: Westminster Press, 1983.

In searching for a genuine Christian spirituality, Pannenberg, one of the world's foremost religious scholars and professor of systematic theology at the University of Munich, writes: "The rediscovery of the Eucharist may prove to be the most important event in Christian spirituality of our time." Eucharistic piety conceived on the basis of the communal symbolism of the Eucharist liberates the Christian from individualism on the one hand and from an overemphasis on the legal authority of ecclesiastical institutions on the other. Pannenberg sees the celebration of the Eucharist to be of central importance for the process of Christian reunification. 115 pages.

Pennington, M. Basil. *The Eucharist Yesterday and Today.* New York: Crossroad, 1984. (Out of print.)

Pennington is a Trappist monk and priest of St. Joseph's Abbey in Spencer, Massachusetts. This book provides a step-by-step treatment of the various parts of the mass, lifting up the heritage of the past and suggesting ways that the heritage can be handed on as something living and life-giving. The style is clear and personal. The author's broad knowledge and keen appreciation of the shape and role of the liturgy in other times and other places laces the content with both information and inspiration. 140 pages.

Saliers, Don E. *Worship and Spirituality.* Philadelphia: Westminster Press, 1984.

In a day when congregations still are visibly polarized into grudging factions over what constitutes true worship, books like this one by Don Saliers, professor of theology and liturgics at Emory University in Atlanta, are needed to foster a new awareness of how the power of Christian worship can transform and renew human lives in this world. Saliers witnesses that Christian worship and spirituality center on "the communal memory of those gathered about the [baptismal] font, the book [the Holy Word], and the table [eucharist]. Without living remembrance of the whole biblical story there would be no authentic worship, nor could there be such a thing as becoming a living reminder of Jesus Christ for others." 114 pages.

Thurian, Max. *The Mystery of the Eucharist.* Grand Rapids, Mich.: Wm. B. Eerdmans, 1984. (Out of print.)

Originally published in 1981 in French, this small volume by Max Thurian of the Täize Community in France holds up the vision of eventual visible unity around the eucharistic table on the part of all who believe in the eucharistic presence of Christ. He traces the development of the Eucharist from the Jewish Passover meal, reviews the different conceptions of the real presence (literalist, metabolist, sacramentalist, realistic, substantialist, and conception of the mystery of the concomitance), and includes a collection of ancient and modern eucharistic prayers from the many branches of the Christian church. 83 pages.

7 | Solitude and Prayer

eister Eckhart said, "Nothing in all creation is so like God as stillness."

When told he handled notes beautifully, a pianist responded: "The notes I handle like all other pianists; the beauty is in the pause between the notes." Silence. Solitude.

Rushing and running—that's our life-style. We've been programmed since birth to hurry. "Hurry and finish your cereal." "Hurry up and get dressed, or you'll be late." "Come on. Come on. Everyone is waiting."

Is it any wonder that we gulp our lunch? The fast-food establishments that line our boulevards simply provide the instant service we require.

A beatitude for our day seems to be "Blessed is that person who can do two things at once." Brush your teeth while you're showering. Watch TV while reading the paper. Open your mail while answering the phone. Plan your next day while making love. Read the back of the bulletin while listening to the sermon.

Few, if any of us, can realize how much the tempo of life has changed us—how much the speed of it is hostile to our spirit. Someone once complained to me: "Al, I spend so much time getting from where I am to where I have to go, I don't have any time to stay where I want to be." Speed, not religion, is our opiate.

The word *haste* in Old English–Saxon once meant *violence*. The meaning has changed but the effect is the same. Haste is violence to our health, to our marriages, to our friendship, to our prayer life. We deplore violence on the screen and in the streets, but we seem to promote haste at home and at church, rushing on the road and hurrying through our prayers.

The title of a magazine article was, "The Greatest Scarcity of Our Times." The next line revealed that *silence* was the resource in question.

Solitude and prayer-time alone were important to Jesus. Why is it, I wonder, that we seem more ready to follow Jesus into service than into solitude? Especially before important decisions were to be made, the Bible shows that Jesus took time to be alone with his Father and to reflect before deciding to move to another locale for ministry, before choosing the disciples, before embracing the cross.

What is there about solitude that brings such nurture and balance to the soul? Why is it that our finest plans and projects are conceived and incubated in the womb of a prayerful, discerning heart? How is it that we are better able to be present to others in their need after we have had occasion to sift through our own confusions in silence? Why do we have to shut down our word-making apparatus to learn better the secret language of eye and hand and heart? What is there about solitude and prayer that helps to open us to truth?

For Further Reading

Baillie, John. *A Diary of Private Prayer*. New York: Charles Scribner's Sons, 1979.

This book includes prayers suited to private use for all the mornings and evenings of the month, plus two prayers for Sunday that may be substituted or added. On the blank left-hand pages is space for petitions and intercessions of the one who prays. Content is widely embracive in scope and profound in spiritual awareness and insight; language is rich in imagery; format is noted for clarity and striking parallelism. It is an enduring aid for those who desire prayers in the thee, thou, art, and "est" tradition. 135 pages.

DelBene, Ron (with Herb Montgomery). *The Breath of Life: A Simple Way to Pray*. Minneapolis: Winston Press, 1981.

Ron DelBene, an Episcopal priest who gives much attention to spiritual direction and teaching others the breath prayer, shares here his counsel for how "to have on the lips what is always in the heart." The breath prayer is a short, simple ancient prayer of praise and petition that usually arises out of our present concern. When practiced with discipline, it can help bring us closer to an awareness of living in the presence of God. 97 pages.

Freeman, Laurence. *Light Within: The Inner Path of Meditation.* New York: Crossroads, 1987.

Typically we believe that supreme effort and determination to achieve are the measures of our success and that nothing can happen without either muscle power or force of will. Father Laurence, prior of the Benedictine Priory of Montreal, lifts up the values of returning to the silent and the empty where we find the sources and ways of strength—not by means of self-improvement, self-analysis, or self-fascination, but by leaving self behind, letting go, and learning to receive grace, hope, and joy. Freeman provides counsel on using a mantra to aid meditation. The book probably is best used in conjunction with spiritual direction. 115 pages.

Hays, Edward. *Pray All Ways.* Easton, Kans.: Forest of Peace Books, 1981.

How does one pray always without learning also to pray all ways? Father Hays challenges us to explore common and ordinary things in our lives as the "stuff" from which are made whole and holy people. How does one do it? He invites: pray with the eyes; pray through the nose; pray with your feet. Plus there is "Feasting as Prayer," "Play as Prayer," and "The Prayer of Tears." Many years of experience as a teacher and pastor, including work with American Indians and experiences in the Near and Far East, give rich texture to Hay's urgings of how to be awake to the reality of the Divine Presence in every aspect of our lives. 164 pages.

Holmes, Marjorie. *I've Got to Talk to Somebody, God: A Woman's Conversations with God.* New York: Bantam Books, 1982.

This book is a collection of conversations with God by a woman for other women on such diverse topics as housework (making beds, peeling potatoes, cleaning the refrigerator), friendship (unexpected company, the childless couple, the coffee klatch), the family (rescue this child, when a husband loses interest, a boy's first car). Women who work out of the home may be looking for a sequel touching in an equally heartfelt and moving way on the kind of issues that fill their days. 121 pages.

Hulme, William E. *Celebrating God's Presence: A Guide to Christian Meditation.* Minneapolis: Augsburg, 1988.

Christian meditation is a specific kind of prayer with its own unique tradition within the Judeo-Christian heritage. It is, as Bill Hulme demonstrates, holistic prayer in that it utilizes body, mind, and spirit while keeping focus on the Word of God as it is recorded in the Scriptures. Part of the Christian Growth Books series, this volume accents prayer as listening, includes a guided meditation, and urges the practice of Bible memorization in an epilog entitled, "Soaked in the Scriptures." Dr. Hulme is professor of pastoral care and counseling at Luther Northwestern Theological Seminary in St. Paul, Minnesota. 124 pages.

Keating, Dr. Charles J. *Who We Are Is How We Pray: Matching Personality and Spirituality.* Mystic, Conn.: Twenty-Third Publications, 1987.

Dr. Keating emphasizes the pleasure, the joy, and the sense of peace that can be ours when we pray out of who we are, rather than against who we are. He uses eight personality characteristics found by Carl Jung and Isabel Briggs Myers (introverted/extroverted; intuitive/sensing; feeling/thinking; judging/perceiving) and relates those traits to spirituality options. In chapter 12 he provides prayer formats for each of the 16 Myers-Briggs personality types. The book includes a helpful index. 147 pages.

Merton, Thomas. *Praying the Psalms.* Collegeville, Minn.: The Liturgical Press, 1956.

In 45 swift pages Merton honors the Psalms as our most perfect book of prayer. "There is no aspect of the interior life, no kind of religious experience, no spiritual need . . . that is not depicted and lived out in the Psalms" (p. 44). The psalms contain cries of wonder, exultation, anguish, or joy. They are youthful and direct, rugged and sober, and they call for zeal, strength, and perseverance. Psalms are songs without plan, Merton maintains, because there are no blueprints for ecstasy. They are full of praise directed Godward. There is one fundamental religious experience that the psalms can teach us, contends Merton: the peace that comes from submission to God's will and from perfect confidence in God.

Muto, Susan Annette. *Meditation in Motion.* Garden City, N.J.: Doubleday and Co., 1986.

Susan Muto, associated with the Institute of Formative Spirituality at Duquesne University in Pittsburgh, celebrates the richness of the ordinary by calling attention to the possibility of being receptive to the "more than" amid the mundane. In an accessible and anecdotal style, she illustrates the many chances sprinkled throughout our day to pause and pray. Such "prayerful presence" puts one in tune with the pulse and pace of grace and engenders peace, justice, and love. Simple, profound, and practical, the book convinces that no matter how busy we are, we can find moments for reflection, refreshment, and renewal. 140 pages.

Postema, Donald H. *Space for God: The Study and Practice of Prayer and Spirituality.* Grand Rapids, Mich.: Bible Way (Board of Publication of the Christian Reformed Church), 1983.

A sabbatical provided Don Postema time to pursue study "toward a Reformed understanding of spirituality." This study course, intended "for busy people who also want to be deep," was the result. It is arranged in nine chapters, all of which begin with reflections on a topic, followed by readings called "Windows to Insight" (Scripture, hymns, and other selections) and finally some exercises, some of which call for journaling. Topics range from "Prayer as Attitude: The Grateful Heart" to "Prayer and Justice/Compassion." Artwork enhances the attractive workbook design. 205 pages.

Quoist, Michel. *Prayers.* Kansas City: Sheed, Andrews and McMeel, 1985.

This is one of very few volumes of prayers for modern Christians that has become a best seller. Quoist is a French priest who received his doctorate in social and political sciences. Believing that we should pray as relevantly as we try to live, he decided to pray about the stuff of modern life more as a friend talking to a friend than by framing remote topics in the archaic, stilted phrases of the usual prayer book. The book was originally published in 1963, but the prayers don't sound out-of-date. They are appreciated in at least nine languages. 179 pages.

Savary, Louis M. and Patricia H. Berne. *Prayerways: For those who feel discouraged or distraught, frightened or frustrated, angry or anxious, powerless or purposeless, overextended or underappreciated, burned out or just plain worn out.* San Francisco: Harper & Row, 1980. (Out of print.)

All the prayerful strategies presented in this book share a common purpose: to help one live a more fully functioning life on all three levels—body, mind, and spirit. The authors report that while we are conscious most often of enduring physical and emotional stresses, we tend to forget the need to nourish the spiritual system, which could support the other two. They assert that the call of holiness and the call to wholeness ultimately are simply different aspects of the same limitless and ever-expanding call. The book contains sound provocative counsels. 161 pages.

Wood, Robert. *A Thirty-Day Experiment in Prayer: Beginning a Prayer Journal.* Nashville: The Upper Room, 1978. (Out of print.)

Thirty days is the classic time for testing one's self in a new mode of living. Robert Wood, director of Spiritual Formation in the Family on the Upper Room staff, believes that keeping a prayer journal can be vital to spiritual formation, so he provides a workbook for the reader's own 30-day experiment in journal writing. For each day he provides themes, Scripture references, prayers, reflection/action queries, and space for morning and evening journaling. 137 pages.

8 | Formative Reading

Formative reading is the kind of reading that nourishes the life of the spirit. Contrast that with other more typical approaches to reading. Often our approach is informational as we look for ideas and facts to enlighten the mind. Or our approach may be recreational as we just relax and enjoy the story line. At times our approach may be literary as we appreciate or analyze the text for its intrinsic quality and attributes. Or again, our approach may be exegetical when we try to understand the ancient text in its "there and then" meaning.

Formative reading is slowed down and reflective. It is inspirational rather than informational, and more qualitative than quantitative.

Formative reading calls for an attitude of receptivity, the grace of appreciation, and participatory engagement.

The chief requirement of formative reading is to move from a mainly argumentative, rationalistic fault-finding mentality to an appreciative, meditative, confirming mood. We are called to move past challenging or rebuffing the text to a savoring of its timeless values. We are called to listen with inner ears of faith to what God may be saying or doing.

Formative reading calls for a posture of docility and humility as we accept the gift of enlightenment coming from beyond our control. We expect not only to be touched by what is read, but transformed by it.

The good news about God's loving us in Christ is not something we intuited. It was revealed to us in God's Word. Attending to that Word, under the counsel of the Holy Spirit, is essential for Christian spirituality. In Holy Scripture and the variety of devotional writings developed in Christianity over the centuries, the Lord leads us to the well of refreshment and love that is God's own spirit. Holy Scripture is the first and primary source of spiritual reading, though scripture reading may effectively be mingled with readings from other Judeo-Christian sources.

When we read Scripture we allow the words to evoke growth. We look for connections to coalesce, for beliefs already held to be confirmed, for hidden meanings to be revealed, for imagination to elaborate and extend the "givens," and for grace to attend to the call to holiness. It's a discipline worth practicing.

For Further Reading

Bangley, Bernard. *Spiritual Treasure: Paraphrases of Spiritual Classics.* New York: Paulist Press, 1985.

Here in everyday language are selections of Western spiritual classics from Augustine, Bernard of Clairvaux, Francis of Assisi, Brother Lawrence, Teresa of Avila, François de Fénelon, and François deSales. Bernard Bangley, pastor of the Quaker Memorial Presbyterian Church in Lynchburg, Virginia, set out to prepare "honestly representative condensations that could be read aloud to the uninitiated in less than an hour." Purists will scoff. I find the work to be worthy of commendation. 131 pages.

Barclay, William. *Daily Celebration.* 2 vols. Waco, Tex.: Word Books, 1971–1973. (Out of print.)

In these two volumes, William Barclay, a prolific writer/preacher of the Church of Scotland, provides a devotional for each day of the year. One doesn't have to be a Barclay fan to marvel at the breadth and depth of these readings, which draw on biblical, literary, and experiential resources. Searchers expecting to find a Bible passage and prayer as part of each exhibit will be disappointed. Persons who want to spend a little time with someone who knows about

life and how it is to be lived will be blessed by looking here. Vol.
I, 316 pages; Vol. II, 285 pages.

Brunner, Emil. *Faith, Hope, and Love*. Philadelphia: Westminster
    Press, 1956. (Out of print.)
    Brunner's title contains three key words central in Christian
experience. Each expresses the whole of Christian existence because
each expresses the relation to Jesus in a particular dimension of
time: *faith* relates to the past, *hope* to the future, and *love* to the
present. Christ says: I carry your past; I am your future; I am the
love in which you now abide. Faith is the hand by which we receive
love. Hope expects what faith believes. Both faith and hope have
their real content in the love of God revealed in Christ. This volume
contains three addresses by a world-renowned theologian. 79 pages.

Chambers, Oswald. *My Utmost for His Highest*. New York: Ballan-
    tine, 1989.
    This is an inspirational classic, originally published in 1935, that
has gone through multiple editions and scores of printings (my copy
is from the fifty-third printing). Chambers, described by one of his
friends as "a great evangelical mystic, a great expositor, and a great
evangelist—but above all a man great in spiritual stature," provides
a one-page reading for each day in the year, based upon scriptural
texts. It is simple, personal, straightforward, and Christ-centered.
A useful index of subjects and an index of biblical references are
included. 375 pages.

Connolly, Finbarr. *God and Man in Modern Spirituality*. Westminster,
    Md.: Christian Classics, 1977. (Out of print.)
    This book results from years of lecturing on spirituality in semi-
naries and other communities in India. Connolly sees three parallel
lines of development in Christian spirituality, and they move together in harmony. There is the line of our growth in love, the
line of our growth in poverty of spirit, and the line of our growth
in prayer. No prayer is complete until it actually has been lived.
No part of life is complete until it has been brought into the dialog
of prayer. I find it incongruous, however, that in a book that seeks

to elucidate "modern" Christian spirituality as contrasted with "traditional" spirituality, no attention has been paid to the sexist language. 245 pages.

De Mello, Anthony. *One Minute Wisdom*. Garden City, N.J.: Doubleday and Co., 1985.
Anthony de Mello served, until his recent death, as director of the Sadhana Institute of Pastoral Counseling in Poona, India. His books, including *Sadhana, The Song of the Bird*, and *Wellsprings* have been translated into 20 languages, signaling their popularity and widespread usefulness. His knowledge of psychology, philosophy, and spirituality spans East and West. His story style engages thoughts and feelings, leading from mood to meaning, and from sense to sensitivity. He remains high on my personal list of favorite spiritual mentors. Once discovered, he will enliven your faith as you return often to these transforming sources. 212 pages.

De Mello, Anthony. *The Song of the Bird*. Garden City, N.J.: Doubleday and Co., 1984.
De Mello has assembled 124 stories/parables from a variety of traditions, Eastern and Western, ancient and modern, which illustrate profound realities that bring us into touch with the problems and concerns of everyday life as well as our common spiritual quest. My personal delight in and indebtedness for this resource is indicated by the repeated references to it in Part I of this book. 172 pages.

Garvey, John, ed. *Modern Spirituality: An Anthology*. Springfield, Ill.: Templegate Publishers, 1985.
The great spiritual traditions would all agree that many of the problems that the modern industrial nations tend to categorize as political and economic have roots in the heart—a truth that can be seen clearly only with attention and discipline. That discipline is what spirituality is concerned with, declares Garvey, a regular columnist for *Commonweal*, and is what prompts him to offer a sampling of some of the best modern spiritual writers. Most are Catholic, Orthodox, or Anglican, including Thomas Merton, Karl Rahner, C. S. Lewis, and Metropolitan Anthony Bloom. Several are Jewish, including Martin Buber and Abraham Joshua Heschel,

and one Buddhist, Chogyyam Trungpa. In all, we get 15 packages in 144 pages.

Jersild, Paul. *Invitation to Faith: Christian Belief Today.* Minneapolis: Augsburg, 1978.

Jersild's invitation to faith leads an inquiring person to critical and formative thinking about it. An evangelical and ecumenical spirit pervades the lucid and balanced treatment. This one-volume summary of the Christian faith, in nine chapters, should continue its usefulness for many years. An annotated bibliography, notes, and an index add to its utility. Dr. Jersild serves as Academic Dean at Lutheran Theological Southern Seminary in Columbia, South Carolina. 223 pages.

Kolden, Marc. *Called by the Gospel: An Introduction to the Christian Faith.* Minneapolis: Augsburg, 1983. (Out of print.)

Marc Kolden, associate professor of systematic theology at Luther Northwestern Theological Seminary in St. Paul, Minnesota, presents a basic introduction to the Christian faith intended "for people in congregations." Clarity and conciseness mark the 13 chapters. Suggestions for further reading and questions for discussion enlarge its usefulness. Kolden's concern to relate faith to life is illustrated in his assertion that "the gospel of our justification by faith on account of Christ frees us from ourselves for our neighbors, from the law for the law, and from seeing our jobs as merely drudgery to vocation" (p. 57). 112 pages.

McNeill, Donald P., Douglas A. Morrison, and Henri J. M. Nouwen. *Compassion: A Reflection on the Christian Life.* Garden City, N.J.: Doubleday and Co., 1983.

The book's jacket says it well: "The great news we have received is that God is a compassionate God. The great call we have heard is to live a compassionate life. The great task we have been given is to walk the compassionate way." Three teachers of pastoral theology collaborate in giving shape to compassion: "It is hard work; it is crying out with those in pain; it is tending the wounds of the poor and caring for their lives; it is defending the weak and indignantly accusing those who violate their humanity; it is joining with the oppressed in their struggle for justice; it is pleading for help, with all possible means, from any person who has ears to hear and eyes to see. In short, it is a willingness to lay down our lives for our friends" (p. 141). 142 pages.

Mitchell, Henry H. and Nicholas Cooper Lewter. *Soul Theology: The Heart of American Black Culture.* San Francisco: Harper & Row, 1986.

What are the healing affirmations that have sustained the Afro-American community through history? What are their central beliefs—enshrined as much in streetwise soul culture as in black preaching—that undergird and sustain American black experience? After 10 years of research and reflection, the authors define 10 components that make up the nourishing spirituality of folk faith. Both informative and inspiring, the work helps people equip themselves with an adequate, biblically based core belief system so they can become and remain emotionally and spiritually whole. 176 pages.

Muto, Susan Annette. *A Practical Guide to Spiritual Reading.* Denville, N.J.: Dimension Books, 1976.

Adrian van Kaam says in the preface to this book: "No other work of this scope on the topic of spiritual reading is at the moment available anywhere in the world in the field of formative spirituality." Part I contains five guidelines for spiritual reading, obstacles and aids to spiritual reading, and a concrete example of spiritual reading. Part II contains three reading programs on themes such as "Living the Desert Experience," "Here I Am, Send Me," and "Stepping Aside and Starting Again." Part III provides an annotated bibliography divided into four sections: essential, secondary, edifying, and recreative. 243 pages.

Ofstedal, Paul, ed. *Daily Readings from Spiritual Classics.* Minneapolis: Augsburg, 1990.

Are you interested in daily readings which couple commentary on contemporary life with excerpts from the writings of 26 classic spiritual writers? I find the idea appealing and testify that, in this case, the linkage works! This year-long devotional volume begins each two-week section with a brief introductory essay on Augustine, C. S. Lewis, Meister Eckhart, and other writers. It then provides a daily one-page reading which relates some germinal idea from that spiritual classic with Scripture, prayer, and life as we know it. Ideal for either individual reading or for group use, this book would make a splendid gift. 408 pages.

Pelikan, Jaroslav. *Jesus through the Centuries: His Place in the History of Culture*. New Haven: Yale University Press, 1985.

Noted historian and theologian Jaroslav Pelikan examines the images of Jesus cherished by successive ages in the history of western culture. He shares 18 images that have been used to portray Jesus over the last two millennia. How a particular age depicted Jesus tells us much about that age—from rabbi in the first century, to universal man in the Renaissance, to liberator in the 19th and 20th centuries. We also learn how they discovered in the life and teachings of Jesus the answers to fundamental questions of human existence and destiny. The kaleidoscope of images provides a wealth of options for spiritual reflection. 270 pages.

Rahner, Karl. *The Practice of Faith: A Handbook of Contemporary Spirituality*. Rev. ed. New York: Crossroad, 1986.

Karl Lehmann and Albert Raffelt have compiled this book of 65 essays from the large collection of what Rahner called his "works of piety." The theological virtues of faith, love, and hope provide the framework for speaking of the essentials of the spiritual life. Spirituality concerns itself with the query and concern: Since I'm going to die, how should I live? Rahner provides penetrating pastoral help. Here's a book to mark up and return to again and again. 316 pages.

Ripple, Paula. *Growing Strong at Broken Places*. Notre Dame: Ave Maria Press, 1986.

Paula Ripple takes issue with our popular culture's disposition toward the quick fix of immediate pain removal or avoidance. Using stories, images, and insights from history, literature, and the lives of others, she explores the sources and effects of suffering in our lives, leading to the understanding that people in pain can experience growth through their suffering. Pain is best seen not as a purposeless part of our lives to be dismissed as "an intolerable companion," but as "a guide leading us beyond ourselves." This book is for all who struggle while seeking meaning in the pain-filled moments of life. 181 pages.

Sittler, Joseph A. *Grace Notes and Other Fragments.* Philadelphia: Fortress Press, 1981. (Out of print.)

A grace note in music does not carry the main melody but provides appreciated ornamentation. Similarly, the reflections, essays, and fragments in this book bless with their accenting and freshening graces. Sittler always is a delight in his creative bonding of profound thought with memorable expression. As a preacher, pastor, professor, and author, Sittler was admired by many. He is especially to be remembered for his concern for nature, earth, created order, and ecology before First Article theology gained wider recognition. 126 pages.

Sittler, Joseph. *Gravity and Grace: Reflections and Provocations.* Minneapolis: Augsburg, 1986.

Sittler said he always tested the usefulness of his theological statements by their transmissibility in his preaching. This book contains a sampling of some of the best that passed that test. "The principal work of the ordained ministry is reflection," said Sittler, as one who modeled that beautifully. "Ministers are often dull functionaires," charged Sittler. Again, Sittler is many things, but he is not dull. Linger awhile with this aphoristic style. Let a sage and seer provoke you to faith and risk. 127 pages.

Thielicke, Helmut. *I Believe: The Christian's Creed.* Translated by John W. Doberstein and H. George Anderson. Philadelphia: Fortress Press, 1968. (Out of print.)

Helmut Thielicke is a professor of theology at the University of Hamburg. He is a theologian who teaches the faith through direct proclamation rather than scholarly dogmatics. He faces squarely and honestly the hard questions that still occupy inquirers of the 20th century: What does it mean to believe? Do miracles really happen? Was Christ's resurrection legend or reality? What is the church in which the creed says Christians believe? This is formative reading at its finest. 255 pages.

Trueblood, Elton. *Confronting Christ.* Waco, Tex.: Word Books, 1960. (Out of print.)

This is an older but still valued devotional interpretation of St. Mark, in 60 brief sections, that assists the reader in confronting the Christ of the gospel. Learned exposition is married with engaging style by this well-known Quaker author. 180 pages.

Wainwright, Geoffrey, ed. *Keeping the Faith: Essays to Mark the Centenary of Lux Mundi.* Philadelphia: Fortress Press, 1988.

Fifteen scholars contribute to this volume of essays that interpret the Christian faith in relation to modern intellectual and moral problems. What claims and meaning does the faith we have received assert in a world marked by seismic explosions in knowledge, communications, and destructive weaponry? The essays are provocative, penetrating, disturbing; hence, they are excellent as formative reading. Editor Wainwright is professor of systematic theology at the Divinity School, Duke University, Durham, North Carolina. 399 pages.

9 | Faith in Daily Life

hat is the key to a faith active in love in all the arenas of daily life? A gospel-centered spirituality declares that empowerment for such living and loving is ours in Christ Jesus alone, as shared in the fellowship of the faithful. Jesus said, "I have a baptism to be baptized with" (Luke 12:50)—that is, he has a purpose to accomplish. That purpose is to make us into what we were not and cannot be without him.

To those bent with guilt Jesus brings forgiveness. To those oppressed by life's burdens he brings relief. To the spineless he gives courage. To the judgmental he gives compassion. To the sad he brings joy. To those who feel worthless he uplifts as priceless. To those who are drifting he provides purpose. To the bored he brings the vibrancy of full life.

And all toward what end?

"Beloved, if God so loved us, we also ought to love one another" (1 John 4:11).

"Let no one despise your youth, but set the believers an example in speech and conduct, in love, in faith, in purity" (1 Tim. 4:12).

"We beseech and exhort you in the Lord Jesus, that as you learned from us how you ought to live and to please God, just as you are doing, you do so more and more" (1 Thess. 4:1).

A college student who was having a hard time getting his act together decided to take his frustrations out on God. He went into the university chapel, sat in the front pew, looked heavenward and said, "All we have on this earth are problems and a bunch of dummies who will never figure out how to solve them. Even I could make a better world than this one!" And somewhere from deep inside, the young man heard God's answer: "That's what you're supposed to do."

And, from Martin Luther, writing in 1522, come these words "Concerning Married Life": "Along comes the clever harlot, namely natural reason, looks at married life, turns up her nose and says: 'Why must I rock the baby, wash its diapers, change its bed, smell its odor, heal its rash, take care of this and take care of that, do this and do that? It is better to remain single and live a quiet and carefree life. I will become a priest or a nun and tell my children to do the same.' But what does the Christian faith say? The father opens his eyes, looks at these lowly, distasteful, and despised things and knows that they are adorned with divine approval as with the most precious gold and silver. God, with his angels and creatures, will smile—not because diapers are washed, but because it is done in faith."

For Further Reading

Bachman, John W. *Faith That Makes a Difference*. Minneapolis: Augsburg, 1983. (Out of print.)

John Bachman, a retired Lutheran pastor, seminary professor, college president, church leader, and communications specialist, always has been a bridge builder. Here in twelve brief, interest-holding chapters he elucidates how Christian faith affects our fears, hopes, decisions, and actions. Well chosen examples, together with quotations and anecdotes, make it clear and memorable how faith may be expressed and applied in daily life. "Faith that makes a difference," he writes, "follows the leading of One who knows the way." 126 pages.

Benne, Robert. *Ordinary Saints: An Introduction to the Christian Life.* Minneapolis: Fortress Press, 1989.

This provides a clear and confident sketch of the content and shape of a life that has been claimed by the grace of God in Christ and is lived out in faith, love, and hope within the places of responsibility that have been given. Hence the title of this solid work by Robert Benne, Jordan-Trexler Professor of Religion at Roanoke College. Ordinary people become ordinary saints not because of either their heroic or ordinary deeds, but because of saving grace received and enabling grace lived out. This book is confessional, contemporary, and comprehensive. 214 pages.

Bonhoeffer, Dietrich. *Life Together,* San Francisco: Harper & Row, 1976.

Here's a quotable classic about Christian community, ministry, and discipleship by the now-famous theologian who was martyred by the Nazis in 1945. Growing out of reflection on his experience as head of a seminary of the German "Confessing Church" on the eve of World War II, this manual for Christian living provides practical guidance relating faith with life. It contains 112 pages of Spirit-enriched witness borne out of blood and tears.

Braaten, Carl E. *Eschatology and Ethics: Essays on the Theology and Ethics of the Kingdom of God.* Minneapolis: Augsburg, 1974. (Out of print.)

Carl Braaten, theologian at Lutheran School of Theology at Chicago, has been one of the most persistent and insightful voices linking biblical faith and ethics to the whole spectrum of urgent current concerns. Trenchant critique is coupled with theologically grounded vision. He speaks with clarity and courage. Six essays on a theology of the Kingdom of God constitute Part I. Part II contains six essays on the ethics of the Kingdom of God. 192 pages.

Brown, L. David. *Take Care: A Guide for Responsible Living.* Minneapolis: Augsburg, 1978.

A caring Lutheran bishop calls us to caretaking "response-ability" because God has called us to care. He emphasizes caretaking of the earth, being better stewards of our bodies, and stripping down our own life-style so we can provide better for the great masses of the poor as we look to the consummate caretaker, Jesus, the Christ. David Brown helps to rehabilitate a strong word: *caring.* 142 pages.

Burtness, James H. *Whatever You Do: An Essay on the Christian Life.*
Minneapolis: Augsburg, 1967. (Out of print.)
This book still is useful as a guide that brings theological thinking
on ethical decisions to people without theological training. Four
chapters treat the seriousness, the ambiguity, the direction, and the
resources of the Christian life. It represents clear thought and con-
cise expression. Burtness continues as professor of systematic theology at Luther Northwestern Seminary in St. Paul, Minnesota.
124 pages.

Carmody, John. *Holistic Spirituality.* New York: Paulist Press, 1984.
John Carmody of Wichita State University in Kansas touches all
the major domains of human existence (nature, society, the self,
and God) with his dual intent to emphasize the centrality of God's
love and the interconnectedness of the different dimensions of the
ordinary believer's life. The author sees economics, politics, ecology,
and local community life as candidates for Jesus' twofold commandment of love. He explores the spiritual potential in diet,
health, exercise, sexuality, education, play, family, and even pain.
He stresses the positive and encouraging side of Christian faith as
touching all components of ordinary living. Here's a book of spiritual
theology that makes concrete the challenges of Christian living
today. 145 pages.

Curran, Dolores. *Traits of a Healthy Family.* San Francisco: Harper
& Row, 1984.
Few of us need more critiques of what is wrong with families.
Nationally recognized columnist, educator, and author Dolores Curran instead heralds what's right in families and shows families how
to build on their strengths to produce even healthier relationships.
Fifteen traits are identified. There are few surprises—just lots of
helpful clarification on topics such as communicating, respecting
others, fostering responsibility, teaching morals, enjoying traditions,
and sharing religion. 280 pages.

Huebsch, Bill. *A Spirituality of Wholeness: The New Look at Grace.*
Mystic, Conn.: Twenty-Third Publications, 1988.
Bill Huebsch, pastoral administrator of the Church of St. Stephen
in Anoka, Minnesota, believes "we really do not learn grace as

much as we are formed in it." He wants readers to understand how a gracious God already is moving in their lives, and to that end unfolds the events and behaviors of everyday life until they become transparent conveyors of grace. The sense-line format he uses sharpens immediate awareness of the coordination and subordination of ideas and gives the work a poetic look and feel. 160 pages.

Kane, Thomas A. *The Healing Touch of Affirmation*. Whitinsville, Mass.: Affirmation Books, 1976.

Affirmation, rather than rigid formation, provides the key to Christian growth and development, argues Father Kane, asserting that it is needed for wholeness and holiness. "The greatest good we do to others is not to give them of our wealth but to show them their own." Affirmation can be visual, such as a responsive smile; it can be tactile, such as an embrace; it can be auditory, such as an expression of sympathy; and it can be spiritual, such as shared prayer. Kane is an educator, priest, and psychotherapist. 126 pages.

Larson, Bruce. *A Call to Holy Living: Walking with God in Joy, Praise, and Gratitude*. Minneapolis: Augsburg, 1988.

Bruce Larson, senior pastor of University Presbyterian Church in Seattle, Washington, and an author, lecturer, and leader in church renewal, shows how God's call to holy living relates both to a radical reshaping of the present world as well as to the kind of personal relationship with a living God that transforms the inner landscape of one's soul, mind, and spirit. Larson links scriptural perspectives from Ephesians, Philippians, and the Gospels with his own engaging style so rich with human stories and fresh language. 126 pages.

Lechman, Judith C. *The Spirituality of Gentleness: Growing Toward Christian Wholeness*. San Francisco: Harper & Row, 1987.

Gentleness, one of the nine fruits of the Spirit, is too easily dismissed in our culture as unreasonable sweetness, powerless passivity, or bland timidity. Lechman, a workshop leader and lecturer, reminds us that the biblical command to be and act with gentleness appears in the Old Testament and New Testament no fewer than 23 times. She speaks of four gifts of the Spirit critical for developing gentleness in our lives: humility, mercy, healing, and giving. Notes and an index are included in its 184 pages.

Logan, Ben, ed. *Television Awareness Training: The Viewer's Guide for Family and Community.* Nashville: Abingdon Press, 1979. (Out of print.)

Violence . . . sex . . . mayhem—and that's only the commercials! What is seeping into our consciousness from incessant television bombardment? How are we being molded without realizing it? Ben Logan, a broadcast producer with United Methodist Communications, tells viewers *how* to watch rather than *what* to watch. Here in workbook format is a book of helps for people who are concerned about how faith in daily life relates to the world of video. 280 pages.

Muto, Susan Annette. *Pathways of Spiritual Living.* 2nd ed. Petersham, Mass.: St. Bedes, 1988.

Associated with the Institute of Formative Spirituality at Duquesne University in Pittsburgh for more than 25 years, Susan Muto contends that the call to holiness entails maintaining a fervent spiritual life in the midst of daily pursuits. Among the "foundations of spiritual formation" that this laywoman addresses are chapters on silence, solitude, prayer, liturgical celebration, spiritual reading, journaling, meditation, contemplation, and serving God in the world. "Most of life occurs in the ditches and trenches of pedestrian routine," contends Muto, as she offers limited guidelines for a distinctively *lay* spirituality lived for the kingdom in the midst of the world. Twelve brief chapters would lend themselves admirably to study and discussions by a small group. 190 pages.

Puls, Joan. *Every Bush Is Burning: A Spirituality for Today.* 2nd ed. Mystic, Conn.: Twenty-Third Publications, 1986.

The title says it. Spirituality must be related to our day-to-day living where we learn to see that "every bush is burning." We are not to retreat from the often harsh realities of our world, says this Franciscan nun, but to enter into them with the confidence that God is present and calls for our presence amid them. A spirituality for our times embodies worship and prayer in the midst of the struggle for justice and peace. To settle for one without the other is to accept a lopsided and limited spirituality, narrowly focused on a one-dimensional God. This book has excellent content and format for small group use. 102 pages.

Puls, Joan. A *Spirituality of Compassion*. Mystic, Conn.: Twenty-Third Publications, 1988.

This is a sequel to Sister Joan Puls's earlier work, *Every Bush Is Burning*. Sample her writing: "We must offer ourselves as places of hospitality and exchange. Letting go of personal wounds to welcome the one who symbolizes our displacement. Turning our physical pain into opportunities for our own and other's growth. Converting brokenness into forgiveness and healing, and failures into expanded sight and sensitivity. Losing some of our prejudices and opening ourselves to new truths. Replacing our need for recognition and honor with anonymous and uncelebrated solidarity" (p. 24). Her perspectives on compassion evolved from her ministry in an inner-city parish, missionary service in India, and a lengthy association with the World Council of Churches headquartered in Geneva, Switzerland. 134 pages.

10 | Spiritual Guides & Spiritual Friends

merican Protestants find a double hindrance to becoming leagued with spiritual companions. Prideful individualism has been given heroic welcome in our culture. Couple that with a distorted understanding of the priesthood of all believers that has many pretending that "they don't need nobody nohow" to assist or even accompany them on the spiritual pilgrimage. Taken together, it's as though the patron saint of American Protestants is like the adventurer who crossed the Atlantic Ocean alone on a surfboard.

It has been noted well that one doesn't have to be sick to get better. Either as a carefully coordinated adjunct to therapy or as a chosen pathway to broader spiritual health, spiritual guides and friends may be the gift waiting to be reclaimed.

The book of Acts gives numerous examples of how the early Christian church provided spiritual guidance through its corporate life and fellowship. Many, including I, have more experience with spiritual direction provided by a group than by a designated person.

Spiritual directors and guides offer widely contrasting approaches. The spiritual director I focus on for illustrative purposes begins her sessions with a period of silence. Both director and directee need some decompression time to attain interior quiet. The directee then tells the director whatever he wants to tell her about his recent spiritual journeying and prayer life. She listens attentively, points out connections she sees in the narrative, questions gently as a way to invite more complete sharing at points, probes on occasion when blockages or evasions are evident, makes suggestions for further reflection, meditation, and prayer, and prays with and for the directee.

The spiritual director is emphatic in denying primary responsibility for another's spiritual growth, as though holding some key of privileged knowledge or spiritual maturity that can guarantee spiritual maturing in another. A spiritual director says both verbally and through her demeanor that the task of both is to attend to that true Counselor, the Holy Spirit, who is always at work at deep levels. Reverence before that formative mystery sets the tone of the encounter, keeps suggestions from being heard as spiritual mandates, and helps to prevent spiritual befriending from becoming a potentially crippling dependency.

Most directors and directees find that 50 minutes to an hour (seldom, if ever, more than one- and one-half hours) is an adequate time frame, if the sharing remains somewhat disciplined. Time intervals between sessions vary from two to four weeks, with three being an average many find compatible.

Spiritual direction should not be seen as a luxury reserved for a special elite. The blessings are there for all willing to embrace its disciplines.

Interestingly, Leroy T. Howe, professor of theology and pastoral care at Perkins School of Theology at Southern Methodist University, suggests that we think of our dreams as spiritual friends. He writes: "Spiritual friendship is the *milieu* in which our dreams occur. Rightly experienced, they come to us as gifts from a friend."[2] Dreams as gifts from a friend? Or are we more disposed to dismiss dreams as alien intrusions into our otherwise normal and settled lives?

Clearly, the topic of spiritual guides and spiritual friends is more far-reaching than we might think at first. Its exploration is both fascinating and rewarding.

For Further Reading

Bonhoeffer, Dietrich. *Spiritual Care.* Translated by Jay C. Rochelle. Philadelphia: Fortress Press, 1985.

In the last forty years, pastoral care has been dominated by psychological methods and language. Here's a handbook in which Bonhoeffer provides a theological base for pastoral theology. In this reexamination of an older *Seelsorge* tradition, theological substance is wedded with practical advice on how to exercise spiritual care in home visitation, conversations with the indifferent, spiritual care to those who are tempted, spiritual care to the sick and dying, as well as ministry at baptisms, funerals, and weddings. Jay C. Rochelle, assistant professor of worship and Dean of the Chapel at the Lutheran School of Theology in Chicago, provides the translation and a helpful, extended introduction. 93 pages.

Bryant, Charles V. *Rediscovering the Charismata: Building Up the Body of Christ through Spiritual Gifts.* Waco, Tex.: Word Books, 1986. (Out of print.)

The church has a great unemployment problem. Charles Bryant, who is a United Methodist pastor, would like to help tens of thousands of church people identify and use their God-given spiritual gifts for the growth of the kingdom. After discussing what the gifts are and are not, he reviews 27 spiritual gifts that usually are encountered in the literature of spiritual gifts. But then he adds, in chapter nine, such "special gifts" as singleness, exorcism, music, witnessing, and missionary vocation. One doesn't have to agree with Bryant on all matters to benefit from this volume. 172 pages.

Clemmons, William P. *Discovering the Depths: Guidance in Personal Spiritual Growth.* Rev. ed. Nashville: Broadman Press, 1987.

The author understands spiritual formation not as a reduction of human life to the spiritual, but as an integration of all dimensions of human personality around the most fundamental dimension— that of our being made in the image and likeness of God. Nor is spiritual formation seen as seeking to make one conform to a predetermined mold. It is more a journey into deeper and deeper dimensions of what it means individually and collectively to be God's people in a world like ours. Dr. Clemmons is professor of Christian education at Southeastern Baptist Theological Seminary in Wake Forest, North Carolina. 138 pages.

The Cloud of Unknowing. Garden City, N.Y.: Doubleday and Co., Image Books, 1973.

An unknown mystic of the 14th century is credited with this first spiritual guide written in Middle English. God can be loved but God cannot be thought. God can be grasped by love but never by concepts. In contemplative prayer, as taught by this director of souls, all thoughts, all concepts, all images must be buried beneath a cloud of forgetting while our naked love (naked because it is divested of thought) must rise upward toward God, who is hidden in the cloud of unknowing. The 75 brief chapters are best read in sequence. 243 pages.

Edwards, Tilden. *Spiritual Friend: Reclaiming the Gift of Spiritual Direction.* New York: Paulist Press, 1980.

What the Roman Catholic and Anglican traditions call "spiritual director" Tilden Edwards names "spiritual friend." As director of the Shalem Institute for Spiritual Formation in Washington, D.C., this Episcopal priest and ecumenical educator provides a substantive framework of historical, theoretical, and practical considerations for shaping the support and guidance that one Christian can give to another over time. Here's reliable help for those curious about or seeking to reclaim the gift of spiritual direction. 264 pages.

Groeschel, Benedict J. *Spiritual Passages: The Psychology of Spiritual Development.* New York: Crossroad, 1983.

To strive for originality in the field of spiritual development strikes Father Groeschel as impertinent. Instead, he seeks to fashion "a useful synthesis" between the doctrines of Christian spiritual tradition and "the more tested and realistic insights of that potpourri called modern psychology." Part II of this informational book provides a psychological understanding of the three ways: The Purgation, The Illuminative Way, and The Unitive Way. Benedict Groeschel is director of the Office for Spiritual Development of the Archdiocese of New York and teacher of pastoral psychology at several major institutions in the New York metropolitan area. 210 pages.

Hamilton, Neill Q. *Maturing in the Christian Life: A Pastor's Guide.* Philadelphia: The Geneva Press, 1984.

Dr. Hamilton, professor of New Testament at Drew University, provides a biblical and theological resource to complement the more psychological approaches to faith development furnished by Piaget, Kohlberg, and Fowler. Based on the assumption that the fundamental aim of the ordained ministry is "to guide parishioners toward maturing in the Christian life," Hamilton argues that "prophetic guide" is the metaphor that can help clergy remember their main role. My copy of the book is well-marked and much-appreciated. Appendix II provides format for a "Faith History Interview," an idea whose time has come. 192 pages.

Kelsey, Morton T. *Companions on the Inner Way: The Art of Spiritual Guidance.* New York: Crossroad, 1983.

Here are guidelines fashioned by an Episcopal priest and counselor for training people who could serve as spiritual companions. They are drawn from elements of three quite different maps: writings of the masters of the devotional life, understandings of the psyche presented by depth psychology, and Kelsey's own "fumbling but persistent" religious practice over four decades. "Those who know the depth of their unworthiness and God's love in spite of it, can best accompany others to the love that transforms," says Kelsey. Chapter 7, "The Personal Journal as a Sacrament of the Inner Journey," is a distillation and extension of his earlier book, *Adventure Inward.* 222 pages.

Koenig, John. *Charismata: God's Gifts for God's People.* Philadelphia: Westminster Press, 1978. (Out of print.)

Editors of *Time* magazine in August 1977 estimated the number of charismatically oriented Christians active in America's traditional churches to be about five million—enough to require that every thoughtful Christian come to terms with charismata. John Koenig, professor of New Testament at Union Theological Seminary in New York City, appeals for a "biblically honest theology of gifts." While acknowledging, "I have never experienced anything so dramatic as a baptism in the Holy Spirit and I do not pray in tongues," Dr. Koenig sees the appearance of charismata in both biblical and modern times as a gracious challenge to the faith-lives of most traditional Christians—his own life included. 213 pages.

Merton, Thomas. *Spiritual Direction and Meditation.* Collegeville,
   Minn.: The Liturgical Press, 1960.
   While allowing that spiritual direction is not necessary for the
ordinary Christian, Merton asserts, "We must not make the mistake
of thinking that direction is a luxury reserved for a special elite."
Spiritual direction, as Merton understands it, has to do with a trusted
friend who, in an atmosphere of sympathetic understanding, helps
and strengthens us in our groping efforts to correspond with the
Holy Spirit, who alone is the true director in the most complete
sense of the word. Part II on meditation acknowledges that meditation cannot be learned from a book. One just has to meditate.
Yet Merton's helps and hints may assist those determined to do
something about a materialistic society that has robbed our nature
of its spiritual energy and tone. 99 pages.

Nemeck, Francis Kelly and Marie Theresa Coombs. *The Way of
   Spiritual Direction.* Wilmington, Del.: Michael Glazier, 1985.
   This study shares, in a helpfully ordered format, insight from
Scripture, from the theological and pastoral traditions of the church,
and specifically from St. John of the Cross and Thomas Merton. I
cite sample outlines from chapters 9 and 10: "Certain tendencies
which may exist within the director impede the listening process.
Those most frequently encountered are: selectivity in listening,
counter-transference, inadequate balance between firmness and
gentleness, and hesitancy to risk" (p. 119). "Certain problems within the directee also tend to obstruct the emergence of spiritual
direction. The principal ones are: unrealistic expectations, pride,
legalism, desire to control the director, undue tension between the
sacrament of reconciliation and spiritual direction, transference and
personality disorders" (p. 130). 220 pages.

Neufelder, Jerome M. and Mary C. Coelho, eds. *Writings on Spiritual
   Direction by Great Christian Masters.* San Francisco: Harper &
   Row, 1982.
   Eccles. 4:9-10 provides some biblical support for spiritual direction. "Two are better than one, because they have a good reward
for their toil. For if they fall, one will lift up the other; but woe to
those who are alone when they fall and have not another to lift

them up." In our struggle to understand our spiritual experiences and hungers, to discern our vocation and to grow toward becoming holy, loving, and loved persons, a guide to confront and inspire may become a true soul friend. Introduction into any art requires a master. Through this anthology of quotations, the masters speak. 205 pages.

Riffel, Herman H. *Voice of God: The Significance of Dreams, Visions, Revelations.* Wheaton, Ill.: Tyndale House Publishers, 1978. (Out of print.)

Even when one cites Scripture and experience, to assert that God will communicate with us personally raises a host of queries, skepticism, and warnings. What about dreams? Visions? How are they to be interpreted? How does one discern the voice of God amid thoughts, impressions, compulsions, or hunches? Morton Kelsey says of it: "This study combines Christian experience, mature biblical understanding and psychological wisdom. I can recommend it to anyone who wants to listen more closely to God. It is not only theoretically sound, but down to earth and practically useful." Pastor Riffel is a graduate of Wheaton College (Illinois) and later studied at the C. G. Jung Institute for analytical psychology in Zurich, Switzerland. 165 pages.

Savary, Louis M., Patricia H. Berne, and Strephon Kaplan Williams. *Dreams and Spiritual Growth: A Christian Approach to Dreamwork.* New York: Paulist Press, 1984.

This work is intended for the reader who is eager to integrate the experiences of dreaming with other aspects of mental and spiritual life. The authors locate themselves solidly in the biblical and Christian tradition in their approach to dreams and visions while incorporating modern psychological insights. The 37 "dreamwork techniques" interspersed throughout the book provide guidelines for dreamwork by spiritual directors, therapists, religious educators, and individuals. 241 pages.

Woodbridge, Barry A. *A Guidebook for Spiritual Friends.* Nashville: The Upper Room, 1985. (Out of print.)

Persons concerned about spiritual growth often discover a need for companionship along the way—a spiritual friend to help them be more accountable for their faith journey. Dr. Barry Woodbridge, pastor of University United Methodist Church in Redlands, California, provides guidance for prayer and conversation shown through the first six times two friends meet to deepen their relationship with God and nurture their spiritual friendship. This book is for those who need explicit help to get started in a spiritual friendship. 93 pages.

11 | Keeping a Personal Journal

A journal is a book in which we carry out the greatest of life's adventures: the discovery of ourselves. The personal journal is a private space of quiet and solitude—a place to befriend ourselves and explore the uniqueness of our life's journey. Henri Nouwen writes in *Sojourners* magazine (March 1987): "Precisely because our secular milieu offers us so few spiritual disciplines we have to develop our own. We have, indeed, to fashion our own desert where we can withdraw every day, shake off our compulsions, and dwell in the gently healing presence of our Lord." A journal, as many will testify, can be just such a desert to which we can withdraw and where we can shake off our compulsions as we dwell in the gently healing presence of our Lord.

For centuries women and men have written journals in times of loneliness, crisis, transition, conflict, spiritual quest, physical or intellectual challenge, or serendipitous joy. In their journals they have found companionship, emotional release, clarification, resolution, the self-affirmation required for courage, the discovery of spiritual resources, and a deeper appreciation of their lives. A journal can be used for many things: to record or chronicle history, to organize one's work, to gather raw materials for writing and speaking, to keep track of the weather or the movement of animals, or to provide an outlet for a wide array of bubblings from within. And, it can be used in faith development.

Journaling as a spiritual discipline is a response to grace, not an alternative to it. Journaling is a way of being open before God, of giving God a chance to work in us. It also can be a means by which we lay hold of the riches of God's mercy.

For me, one of the major benefits of journaling has been to sense repeatedly how grace operates in my life. I see its multiple unfolding patterns and am awed. I ask myself: If such grace has attended me so faithfully in the past, why do I get so uptight and graspy in the present? Why should I not relax more in the flow of such reliable, transcendent caring? Why should I fret as though hostile forces were ultimately in charge? Why should I worry that bland neutrality will cause my life to go into aimless drift unless I forcefully make life happen? Journaling has helped me to see that grace has been my chief attendant thus far and the powers of God's light have illumined my way.

For Further Reading

Cargas, Harry J. and Roger J. Radley. *Keeping a Spiritual Journal.* Garden City, N.Y.: Doubleday and Co., 1981. (Out of print.)

The authors see journaling as a way of being good to yourself. It involves a journey into "inner space" to "uncover bit by bit the great mystery of your life." This readable, activity-oriented paperback is intended to help teenagers start a journal. It is written by teachers who understand youth and the things they need to establish useful new habits. 128 pages.

Casewit, Curtis W. *The Diary: A Complete Guide to Journal Writing.* Allen, Tex.: Argus Communications, 1982. (Out of print.)

This work is a useful guide for beginners and a stimulating source of new ideas for experienced diarists. The author uses the words *journal* and *diary* interchangeably. Sections on honesty, writer's block, and "the diary as indicator of whether or not you need help" may be especially helpful. Curtis Casewit has been associated with the creative writing department of Colorado University in Denver. 146 pages.

Kelsey, Morton T. *Adventure Inward: Christian Growth through Personal Journal Writing*. Minneapolis: Augsburg, 1980.

Morton Kelsey has written and lectured widely on topics in psychology, religion, and education. Here he couples that academic background with more than 30 years of experience as a journal writer. This would serve as a dependable guide for anyone who wishes to keep a religious journal. The work has clear organization, penetrating insights, and balanced treatment. It includes helps for interpreting dreams, along with a bibliography for further reading. 216 pages.

Klug, Ronald. *How to Keep a Spiritual Journal*. Nashville: Thomas Nelson, 1982.

Ronald Klug, a teacher, editor, missionary, and author, has kept a journal for more than 25 years, describing it as "a tool for self-discovery, an aid to concentration, a mirror for the soul, a place to generate and capture ideas, a safety valve for the emotions, a training ground for the writer, and a good friend and confidant." I have with profit used this book as a supplemental text for a seminary course on journaling. It contains a helpful bibliography for further reading on journaling as a spiritual discipline. 142 pages.

Progoff, Ira. *At a Journal Workshop: The Basic Text and Guide for Using the Intensive Journal*. New York: Dialogue House Library, 1977.

Along with Carl Jung, Marion Milner, and Anaïs Nin, Ira Progoff is one of four 20th-century pioneers of psychology and literature who played a major role in conceptualizing the principles of modern journal writing. His system, called the Intensive Journal, is somewhat complex and is best learned by attending one of his journal workshops, after which this text has demonstrable usefulness. More than anyone else, Progoff has brought journal writing as a form of growth work to public attention. I owe my own start as a journal writer to him. Progoff has produced several related spin-off publications the past dozen years. 320 pages.

Rainer, Tristine. *The New Diary: How to Use a Journal for Self-Guidance and Expanded Creativity*. Los Angeles: Jeremy P. Tarcher, Inc., 1978.

Creative, contemporary, and comprehensive, this is the work I return to when my journaling needs some freshening. Well acquainted with the large and growing literature on journaling, Rainer offers numerous possibilities for using the diary to achieve your own purposes. The book contains 323 pages, including an index, and 10 pages of bibliography of interest to diarists.

Santa-Maria, Maria L. *Growth Through Meditation and Journal Writing: A Jungian Perspective on Christian Spirituality.* New York: Paulist Press, 1983.

The author, a psychotherapist in private practice in St. Petersburg, Florida, holds to the Jungian thesis that many psychological problems of adulthood are symptomatic of a deeper spiritual concern, such as a search for life meaning and purpose and, ultimately, a search for God. Our Western society, with its focus upon technology and its excessive use of reason, has brought about an impoverishment of the spiritual life of individuals. This work presents seven dimensions of mature Christian spirituality complete with scriptural references, exercises in guided meditation and journal writing, and brief bibliographic notes for further reading. 157 pages.

Simons, George F. *Keeping Your Personal Journal.* New York: Paulist Press, 1978.

Among the earlier efforts to provide guidelines and suggestions for journal keeping is this modest work by a Catholic clergyperson who is both a journal writer and a leader of journal workshops. Under the title of "Exploring Soul Country," Part II contains 32 pages of exercises useful both for individuals and groups. That section will continue to contribute the most to the ongoing viability of this volume. 144 pages.

12 | Fasting and Other Bodily Disciplines

Richard Foster, one of my most respected spiritual mentors, challenges: "Why has the giving of money, for example, been unquestionably recognized as an element in Christian devotion and fasting so disputed? Certainly we have as much, if not more, evidence from the Bible for fasting as we have for giving. Perhaps in our affluent society fasting involves a far larger sacrifice than the giving of money." And again, "Fasting can bring breakthroughs in the spiritual realm that could never be had in any other way. It is a means of God's grace and blessing that should not be neglected any longer."[2]

The central idea in fasting is the voluntary denial of an otherwise normal function for the sake of more disciplined spiritual living. There is nothing wrong with any normal life functions, but there are times when we set them aside as a religious and/or physical discipline or as a means of protest. When we view fasting from this perspective, we can see its reasonableness as well as its broader dimensions of usefulness.

The list of biblical people who fasted is a veritable "Who's Who" of Scripture, including Moses the lawgiver, Daniel the seer, David the king, Anna the prophetess, Elijah the prophet, Esther the queen, Paul the apostle, and Jesus Christ, the incarnate Son of God.

Keep searching for those who fasted and witnessed to its value in the annals of church history and you'll find John Wesley, John Calvin, John Knox, Martin Luther, Jonathan Edwards, Charles Finney, and a host of others.

Nor is fasting exclusive to the Judeo-Christian heritage. All the major religions of the world recognize its merit. Remember how those foreign Ninevites in the book of Jonah fasted after the prophet preached to them? Zoroaster practiced fasting, as did Confucius, as do the Yogis of India. Plato, Socrates, and Aristotle all fasted. Even Hippocrates, the father of modern medicine, believed in fasting.

Now the fact that all these individuals, in and out of scripture, held fasting in high regard does not make it necessary or even desirable. But perhaps it does for you what it did for me—it allowed me to be willing to look again at some of the popular, largely unexamined assumptions of our day concerning the widely neglected discipline of fasting.

Couple fasting with other bodily disciplines such as good nutrition and regular exercise and ask, Do such matters belong in a book of gospel-centered spirituality? Emphatically yes. It's time we put some *body* into our spirituality. The issue of how western Christianity omits the body from its spirituality is dismaying. "Heretical" would be the stronger word, if we still cared about such matters. The heresy? Neo-docetism. Docetism figured in ancient christological controversies contending that Jesus Christ had only an apparent body and only appeared to suffer and die. Thus, neo-docetism is that tendency, implicit or explicit, to see true Christianity as affecting only the human spirit—that God works only in the depths of the human soul and does not really care about, change, or affect matter in any way. An incarnational spirituality says rather that matter matters. Even as Jesus became human, we are obliged to take our total humanness with seriousness. This includes body and all. Care of the body honors the Creator who fashioned it, the Redeemer who became incarnate, and the Spirit who makes of our body a temple.

For Further Reading

Braaten, Carl E. and LaVonne. *The Living Temple: A Practical Theology of the Body and the Foods of the Earth.* New York: Harper & Row, 1976. (Out of print.)

1

Husband Carl, the theologian, and wife LaVonne, the nutritionist, believe it is time to join what our Western culture has put asunder—theological conviction and nutritional wisdom. They provide a sourcebook for a healthier way to live as they fashion a practical body theology. They assert that a spirituality that prefers spiritual ecstasy over somatic wholeness is sanctimonious humbug. Until junk food is passé, this sensible book deserves ever wider usage.

Campbell, Peter A. and Edwin M. McMahon. *Bio-Spirituality: Focusing as a Way to Grow.* Chicago: Loyola University Press, 1985.

Religion of the head gives rise to an excessively rational tradition of spirituality, assert these coauthors, Roman Catholic priests, and workshop and retreat leaders. They argue we can get to deeper roots of the Spirit than formulated beliefs by a system called *focusing*— a discipline of attending to the bodily "felt-sense" of what is at work in one's life. Focusing makes one attend to areas of hurt and weakness lodged deep in the memories of the body, which forgets nothing. This searching for bodily awareness is in fact a spiritual way of knowing. Appendix 3 articulates the nine "learnings we value in searching for a bio-spirituality." 159 pages.

Cooley, Donald G., ed. *After-40 Health and Medical Guide.* Des Moines: Meredith Corporation, 1980. (Out of print.)

Remarkable advances in medicine, health care, sanitation, housing, nutrition, technology, immunization, surgery, and pharmacology assure a continually increasing proportion of vigorous "over 65s" in our population. In this book sponsored by *Better Homes and Gardens*, specialists share their knowledge and friendly counsel about matters of mind and body that are especially pertinent to the middle and later years of life. Since healthful attitudes, practices, and preventive measures are our own responsibility, access to a guide of this sort may be a helpful supplement to regular medical care. 480 pages.

Cousins, Norman. *Anatomy of an Illness as Perceived by the Patient: Reflections on Healing and Regeneration.* New York: Bantam Books, 1979.

Here's a best-selling story that has been told in major medical and lay journals around the world—Norman Cousins' successful fight against a crippling disease, in partnership with his physicians and all the positive forces of his own being, including laughter, courage, and tenacity. The theme is clear, powerful, and heartening: Every person must accept a certain measure of responsibility for her or his own recovery from disease or disability, and nothing is more remarkable about the human body than its recuperative drive. 173 pages.

Padus, Emrika (and the editors of *Prevention* magazine). *The Complete Guide to Your Emotions and Your Health: New Dimensions in Mind/Body Healing.* Emmaus, Penn.: Rodale Press, 1986.

Health and happiness have long been pursued as dual treasures. Now medical and psychological research points to an inexorable link between the two: happy people are healthier. They are better able to resist stress and ward off cardiovascular disease and gastrointestinal troubles. Their immune systems are less likely to break down and may even work harder, protecting them against allergies, arthritis, and cancer. Their brains are awash with natural pain-relieving chemicals, so they feel better. This work contains more than 700 pages of reports on the latest research and clinical experience of physicians, psychiatrists, and other professionals at the forefront of the new frontier of mind/body health. 732 pages.

Ryan, Regina Sara and John W. Travis. *Wellness Workbook: A Guide to Attaining High Level Wellness.* Berkeley: Ten Speed Press, 1981.

The *Wellness Workbook* is an invitation to a never-ending, every-breath-you-take process of caring for the physical, emotional, intellectual, and spiritual fiber of our lives. It contains a wealth of information designed to cajole, provoke, and stimulate thinking and doing in relation to health and health care. It includes a 300-item self-scoring questionnaire, "The Wellness Index." 236 pages.

Sehnert, Keith W. *Selfcare/Wellcare: What You Can Do to Live a Healthy, Happy, Longer Life.* Minneapolis: Augsburg, 1985.

Keith Sehnert is a pioneer in the medical self-care movement, sharing here the "hows" and "whys" of high-level wellness. As a

Christian medical doctor, he coins the word *wellcare,* combining the concepts of wellness with stewardship of the body/self. This book, along with his earlier best-sellers *Stress/Unstress* (Augsburg, 1981) and *How to Be Your Own Doctor—Sometimes* (out of print), contains a wealth of reliable data presented in graphic, highly practical ways. And while sharing leadership in workshops with Keith and his wife, Colleen, my wife and I observed that he practices what he teaches. For the Sehnerts wellcare is a way of life. 239 pages.

Tubesing, Donald A. and Nancy Loving Tubesing. *The Caring Question: You First or Me First—Choosing a Healthy Balance.* Minneapolis: Augsburg, 1983.

As pioneers in the whole-person health movement, the Tubesings bring to sharp focus the issue of self-care in a life of service. "You can't be healthy unless you care for yourself. You aren't healthy unless you put your health to use for others" (p. 201). Their practical helps include checklists, thought-provoking questions, and space for guided personal reflection. It's a book to be used—not just read. 220 pages.

13 | Simplicity as a Life-style

ost Christians in America never have seriously wrestled with the spiritual discipline
of simplicity. Instead they conveniently ignore Jesus' many words on the subject.

The reason for ignoring simplicity is simple. Spiritual discipline
directly challenges our vested interests in an affluent life-style.

I hope and pray that the Holy Spirit assists us to relax our defenses
enough so that we may consider anew the potential this discipline
might have as we seek God's leading us into the deeper places of
spiritual maturation.

John, the apostle and close friend of Jesus, said: "If any one has
the world's goods and sees his brother [or sister] in need, yet closes
his heart against him [or her], how does God's love abide in him?"
(1 John 3:17). Can we close our eyes and hearts to how we live,
eat, dress, or entertain ourselves and at the same time seek to be
fully one with God? Simplicity of life-style becomes a question of
spiritual import as we allow biblical witness to illumine.

Think of how the "mammon" spirit permeates even our my-
thology. Who among us becomes the modern hero? Why, it's the
poor person who becomes rich! Or the lottery winner who hits it
big! The one who moves, by whatever means, from having little
to having much.

What has happened to the Franciscan or Buddhist ideal of the rich person who voluntarily becomes poor? Who lauds the one who sets aside life's complicating muchness for a heart more devotedly and simply given to life's truly satisfying values? Sad to say, such thinking is relegated by most to the spiritually bizarre edge of cultural appreciation.

Courageously we need to articulate new and more humane ways to live. The spiritual discipline of simplicity has been a recurrent vision throughout history. It doesn't need to remain a lost dream; it can be recaptured. In this case, why should not that which can be, be?

The spiritual discipline of simplicity may be the only safeguard that can sufficiently reorient our lives so that possessions can be genuinely enjoyed without their destroying us.

A changed life-style in the direction of simplicity is a faithful witness to a better way to live at peace.

For Further Reading

Cooper, John C. *Finding a Simpler Life*. Philadelphia: United Church Press, 1974. (Out of print.)

The subject of this book is why and how men and women today are opting out of mainline American culture. A group of new pioneers is seeking a plainer life. They are disturbed and frightened by poverty and unemployment, the residual hatred of the mainline culture by neglected minority groups, and, above all, by the shattered and poisoned earth, air, and water of the continent along with the poisoned political atmosphere impotent to do much about those ills. The new wave of simplicity is composed of people moving from strength in "establishment" terms to strength in terms of their own goals and desires. Therefore the attraction of the plainer life is psycho/spiritual rather than eco/political in its primary foundations. Are we looking at pseudo innocence? To what degree does the yearning for a simpler past represent an opening to the Spirit, and to what degree does it represent a flight from the prophetic demands of justice in the midst of society's trials? Those questions remain as good for the 1990s as they were for the 1970s. 127 pages.

Eller, Vernard. *The Simple Life: The Christian Stance toward Posses-sions.* Grand Rapids, Mich.: Wm. B. Eerdmans, 1973. (Out of print.)
Eller contends that the simple life is the believer's *inner* rela-tionship to God's finding expression in one's *outward* relationship to "things." Both elements need to be kept in view simultaneously. In Part I we find an examination of the simple life as taught by Jesus and company. In Part II the focus falls on Søren Kierkegaard (Denmark, 1813–55), who is believed by Eller to be the major thinker from Christian history to give the most effective attention to "the simple life." Finally, in Part III the author shares his personal witness that Christian simplicity ought not be seen as an anxious scrupulosity about possessions. Rather, when life becomes focused upon God instead of "things," one not only is *freed from* all the anxieties that attend possessions, but one also is *made free to* use "things" with all the blessing and joy for which they were created and given to us in the first place. 122 pages.

Foster, Richard J. *Freedom of Simplicity.* New York: Harper & Row, 1981.
In *Celebration of Discipline* (1978), Foster provided a single chapter on simplicity. In this volume he traces the roots of simplicity through the Bible and the early church, illustrates these principles with examples from the lives of saints, and establishes the relevance of simplicity to modern personal and social ills. He shows how sim-plicity provides us the option to be free and fulfilled and to live with grace, balance, and joy. Urging Christians to make their lives "models of simplicity," he provides a concrete guide to help us rethink our priorities. It's an essential resource for this topic. 200 pages.

Schaeffer, Francis A. *Pollution and the Death of Man: The Christian View of Ecology.* Wheaton, Ill.: Tyndale House Publishers, 1970. (Out of print.)
Modern culture is poor in its sensitivity to nature. It's more than a matter of aesthetics or the avoidance of a problematic future. Contemporary upsets of ecological balance already diminish the quality of life for most. Dr. Francis Schaeffer, director of L'Abri

Fellowship in Switzerland, points out biblical Christian guidelines that would, if followed, bring about substantial healing and restoration. They also would affect a change in our life-styles. 125 pages.

Schramm, John and Mary. *Things That Make for Peace: A Personal Search for a New Way of Life.* Minneapolis: Augsburg, 1976. (Out of print.)
This book is the journal of two people who set out to live what they learned to be true—that peace is a life-style. Their search for and experience with *shalom* led them to explore the issues of non-violence, ecology, world hunger, contemplation, simplicity, and faithfulness in personal relationships. The book doesn't preach but facilitates our painful self-examination as persons, as members of the body of Christ, and as world citizens. 112 pages.

Shi, David E. *The Simple Life: Plain Living and High Thinking in American Culture.* New York: Oxford University Press, 1985.
There is no magical guidebook one can follow to live a simple life. But thanks to David Shi, associate professor of history at Davidson College in Davidson, North Carolina, we do have a scholarly historical tracing of the simple life in the United States. Shi synthesizes many strands of American thought and behavior as he shows how simplicity remains an animating vision of vital moral purpose. He also shows how human nature and the imperatives of the consumer culture constantly war against enlightened restraint. He maintains that a modern simple life, informed by its historical tradition, can be both socially constructive and personally gratifying, even though determining and maintaining the correct degree of simplicity is far from a simple endeavor. 332 pages.

Simple Living Collective (American Friends Service Committee). *Taking Charge: Achieving Personal and Political Change through Simple Living.* New York: Bantam Books, 1977. (Out of print.)
Many people throughout the United States believe that if the world family is to be cared for and fed, the United States must begin wide-scale "dedevelopment." For this to happen, they feel, American citizens must adopt new ways of life in which they consume

only their fair share of the earth's resources. The Simple Living Collective of the American Friends Service Committee is among those believing that how you live can make a difference. The collective provides practical suggestions for change in our daily lives, our communities, and the world. They speak of work, clothing, health care, energy, food, and another view of economics. This work is for all who want to grapple with what it means to be a world citizen and to commit themselves to lead an ecologically sound life. 341 pages.

Taylor, John V. *Enough Is Enough: A Biblical Call for Moderation in a Consumer-oriented Society.* Minneapolis: Augsburg, 1977 (First U.S. edition). (Out of print.)

Enough is Enough represents one of the early but still useful calls to free ourselves from the extravagance and waste of excessive consumption. This eloquent defense of simple living rests on biblical and theological groundwork, but it also moves to provide also some personal and communal strategies for implementing a "life of enough." It was first published in England; the book's author serves as bishop of Winchester. 124 pages.

14 § Seeking Justice for the Oppressed

William Sloane Coffin Jr. has been among leaders calling for the contemporary church to step past charity work and to walk the difficult path to peace and justice. "If you provide food for the hungry you may be considered a saint, but if you ask how come people are going hungry you'll probably be called a Marxist," he said in Columbus. "So churches, in order to maintain their middle-class respectability, are apt to back away from justice in favor of charity. Churches would appear to have a vested interest in unjust structures that produce victims to whom they can then pour out their hearts in charity, thus ensuring the continuance of an ecclesiastical system noted for being long on charity and short on justice."[4]

It has become popular in some quarters to disparage "charity" or "compassion" and to sloganeer about "justice." I believe the two will be linked in a mature spirituality. Certainly they were joined in the life of our Lord.

In the spirit of Jesus, Christians have individually and communally performed "works of mercy." Traditionally, there are seven of them: feeding the hungry, giving drink to the thirsty, clothing the naked, harboring the stranger, visiting the sick, ministering to prisoners, and burying the dead.

But also in the spirit of Jesus it is right that we be provoked to anger and protest by injustice to others, by callous treatment of the weak and the defenseless, and by misuse of religion.

We are to relieve symptoms of injustice while we remove or alleviate causes of hurt. While we work to restore order, we also must work to promote justice. Misused advantage equals injustice. Mishandling blessings is an act of violence sure to provoke violence in response.

We hear that an estimated 15,000 people die of hunger each day while considerably more than 15,000 people grow increasingly restive about a world divided between the overfed and the underfed. The underfed believe that it is truly a violent act for the well-fed to withhold surplus food from them.

A spirituality that contributes to *shalom* sees how the arms race affects the poor and hungry. It dares to ask almost overly simple questions such as: Might not the wise reallocation of resources now devoted to preparing for war give lots of people a chance at life? Isn't it unethical to consume vast wealth for weapons when that wealth is needed to create tolerable life for the millions who live in poverty? Isn't it time to fashion a theology of food? Is a theology of food any less holy than a theology of forgiveness? In following Jesus through a life of responsible discipleship, shouldn't we examine more carefully the accumulation and use of wealth in the midst of poverty and hunger?

The issues are exceedingly complicated, but that's why we must keep asking the hard questions. Our way of life is a violation of Christian fellowship, an assault on the future of humankind. To allow the hungry to remain hungry—the oppressed to remain oppressed—is nothing less than blasphemy against God, for what is nearest and dearest to God is precisely the need of our needy neighbors. Justice is the most God expects of pagans. It is the least God expects of Christians.

For Further Reading

Bernier, Paul. *Bread Broken and Shared: Broadening Our Vision of Eucharist.* Notre Dame, Ind.: Ave Maria Press, 1981.

Paul Bernier, a pastor, professional theologian, and journalist, reminds that Jesus has only one table to which all are called. The sign of the Eucharist is a sign of solidarity. "But," charges Father Bernier, "it has gone from being the ultimate expression of Jesus' gift of self to a needy world, to a harmless ritual which has ceased to challenge us." To live the Eucharist in our daily lives is to be personally and globally transformed, giving us a totally new life of worship, witness, and discipleship. It pledges us to alleviate human suffering and address its causes. 140 pages.

Bonino, José Míguez. *Doing Theology in a Revolutionary Situation.* Philadelphia: Fortress Press, 1975.

Professor Míguez Bonino is dean of post-graduate studies of the Higher Evangelical Institute for Theological Studies in Buenos Aires, Argentina. He identifies with the growing number of Christians in Latin America who are involved in a struggle for economic, social, and cultural liberation. Liberation theologians seeking to be faithful to a down-to-earth Lord invite us to think theologically, in depth before God, about the actual problems that confront them daily. How can the church remain strictly impartial in faith as it serves all sinners alike in its ministry of Word and sacraments and yet be compassionately partial in love as it struggles on behalf of God's suffering "have-nots" in its ministry of mercy and justice? This work presents some challenging questions, unsettling alternate lines of action, and far-reaching implications. 179 pages.

Brown, Robert McAfee. *Spirituality and Liberation: Overcoming the Great Fallacy.* Philadelphia: Westminster, 1988.

The "great fallacy" is, of course, the separation between the spiritual and the temporal; between prayer and social involvement. Brown's thesis: Spirituality is basic to the religious life, but it can be enriched by the contribution of liberation. Liberation is basic to the religious life, but it can be enriched by the contribution of spirituality. Indeed, spirituality when radically understood includes what is meant by liberation. Rabbi Abraham Joshua Heschel understood this. His title at the Jewish Theological Seminary in New York City was professor of mysticism and ethics. Brown gives readers clear arguments, wonderful illustrations, and a colorful and witty style. (On page 35 he uses the word *gallimaufry* and tells you to "look it up"!) 160 pages.

The Challenge of Peace: God's Promise and Our Response: A Pastoral Letter on War and Peace. National Conference of Catholic Bishops. May 3, 1983.

Roman Catholic bishops, in this lengthy 103-page letter, dare to address matters fraught with great complexity, controversy, and passion. They see the nuclear age as an era of moral as well as physical danger, noting that along with the obvious military and political choices, decisions involve fundamental moral choices. Fearing that our world and nation are headed in the wrong direction and desiring to live up to Jesus' call to be peacemakers in our own time and situation, the bishops call for a "moral about-face" in the conviction that a better world is here for human hands and hearts and minds to make.

Gollwitzer, Helmut. *The Rich Christians and Poor Lazarus.* New York: Macmillan Co., 1970. (Out of print.)

Originally published in German in 1968, this volume is a vigorous polemic on poverty and wealth, the threat of world hunger, and modes of effecting social change. We belong to a third of humanity who is concerned with dieting and losing weight, while the other two-thirds are concerned with hunger. Jesus' parable of the rich man and poor Lazarus (Luke 16:19-31) is addressed exclusively to the rich man, charges Gollwitzer. It is not meant to console the poor with hope of recompense beyond the grave, but to warn the rich of damnation and to incite them to hear and act in this world. The aim of the gospel is to console our consciences and, at the same time, to mobilize our consoled consciences to help effect needed political, social, and economic consequences. 108 pages.

Gutierrez, Gustavo. *The Power of the Poor in History.* Translated by Robert R. Barr. Maryknoll, N.Y.: Orbis Books, 1983.

Gutierrez is a pioneer in practicing a theology of liberation, a theology from the bottom, from "the underside," created by the victims, the poor, and the oppressed. It is not theology spun out in a series of timeless theological axioms that are then applied to the contemporary scene. Liberation theology springs up out of the poverty, the oppression, and heartrending conditions under which many Latin Americans live. In this work he presents in eight major essays his developing theological insights since his landmark work *A Theology of Liberation* (out of print), which was published in English a decade earlier. 240 pages.

Halvorson, Loren E. *Peace on Earth Handbook: An Action Guide for People Who Want to Do Something about Hunger, War, Poverty, and Other Human Problems.* Minneapolis: Augsburg, 1976. (Out of print.)

Local and global perspectives, guidelines for what can be done and the encouragements of what has been done, the language of faith and the language of social issues—they're all here in this "scout's report" of one who works the territory between institutions of the church and the frontiers of direct social engagement. Loren Halvorson, who is on the faculty of Luther Northwestern Seminary in St. Paul, Minnesota, has done such scout work and witness for more than 35 years. While some of the illustrations and resource listings clearly are dated, the basic constructs and passion for the enterprise still provide formative helps. 128 pages.

Hellwig, Monika K. *The Eucharist and the Hunger of the World.* New York: Paulist Press, 1976.

This book explores the world's deep-rooted hungers, both spiritual and physical, suggesting how and why they intersect. The central action of the Eucharist, says Monika Hellwig, a professor of theology at Georgetown University in Washington, D.C., is the *sharing* of food—not only the *eating* of it. For most Christians the Eucharist is the center of their religious observance, involving always an act of allegiance, of self-identification, and of commitment. It not only affirms and supports, but also demands and challenges. Indeed, to accept the bread of the Eucharist is to accept being bread and sustenance for the poor of the world. 90 pages.

Jersild, Paul T. and Dale A. Johnson. *Moral Issues and Christian Response.* 4th ed. New York: Holt, Rinehart and Winston, 1988.

How one relates to ethical questions reveals much about one's spirituality. This volume of readings on particular issues is divided into five major sections. The first, dealing with individual and communal aspects of decision making, is an introduction to the others. The four that follow address sexual ethics, minority-group issues, issues of conflict, and the biomedical revolution from a variety of religious and societal perspectives. Some details are now dated, but one still finds adequate stimulation, support, and challenge for one's own thinking. 467 pages.

Matsuki, Suguru, ed. *Testimonies of Hiroshima and Nagasaki: A Resource for Peacemaking.* Translated by Carl and Nijiko Bergh. Fukuyama, Japan: Hajime Kikaku Ltd., 1984.

Believing that Hiroshima and Nagasaki are symbolic events that reveal the result of human sin and call us through faith to repentance, the Committee for Peace and Nuclear Disarmament of the Japan Evangelical Lutheran Church caused to be assembled this collection of testimonies by Lutheran Church members in Japan who survived the bombings. First-person accounts of hellish events are a dramatic means for raising people's consciousness. After "this war of aggression was brought to a close, . . . the Japanese people deeply reexamined themselves, repented, and vowed never again to cause a war. It is clearly stated in the Constitution of our land that Japan will neither use nor maintain military arms for the purpose of war." 101 pages.

Mooneyham, W. Stanley. *What Do You Say to a Hungry World?* Waco, Tex.: Word Books, 1975. (Out of print.)

Stan Mooneyham, president of World Vision International, spends at least two-thirds of each year traveling the world in search of the helpless and needy. Realizing that myths about hunger and starvation are perpetuated by ignorance, he presents facts and figures with clarity and pathos. He invites dialog as he poses hard questions and suggests harder answers. Finally he invites a commitment to care. 272 pages.

Nouwen, Henri J. *Thomas Merton: Contemplative Critic* (originally published with the title *Pray to Live*). San Francisco: Harper & Row, 1981.

Thomas Merton continues to have wide appeal to all types of women and men in varied life situations. Henri Nouwen has made broad and judicious use of Merton's writings, clearly revealing that Merton's social and political critique was based not on public debate and analysis but rather on a contemplative penetration into the heart of God. No one more than Merton showed that the monastic life is not a retreat from reality. Here's a refreshing encounter with the living spirit of Merton. 158 pages.

Pilgrim, Walter E. *Good News to the Poor: Wealth and Poverty in Luke-Acts.* Minneapolis: Augsburg, 1981. (Out of print.)
    Jesus had much to say about possessions and their use. Walter Pilgrim, professor of theology at Pacific Lutheran University in Tacoma, Washington, examines Luke's unique interpretation of Jesus' proclamation of good news to the poor and discusses what that tradition may have to say to affluent Christians and churches in our time. 198 pages.

Shinn, Roger Lincoln. *Forced Options: Social Decisions for the 21st Century.* San Francisco: Harper & Row, 1982.
    Does humanity belong on the endangered species list as it struggles with resource shortages, large-scale ecological imbalances, and the threat of nuclear war? Roger Shinn, Reinhold Niebuhr Professor of Social Ethics at Union Theological Seminary in New York, and adjunct professor of religion at Columbia University, points out the necessity of defining the issues and making decisions now because humanity risks endangerment. Collectively we must seek solid, long-term solutions that address not only complexity but the relevance of ethics and religion as well as technology, economics, and politics in the decision-making process. In 12 chapters, this work is sobering yet hopeful; forthright yet balanced. 267 pages.

Sider, Ronald, ed. *Cry Justice: The Bible on Hunger and Poverty.* New York: Paulist Press, 1980.
    Sponsored by Bread for the World, this book contains biblical texts that pertain to hunger, justice, and the poor. It's designed to assist in the study to which faithful Christians are called: to couple careful assessment of biblical teaching with intelligent analysis of contemporary poverty and its systemic causes. The sheer volume of biblical material that pertains to questions of hunger, justice,

and the poor is astonishing. Organizational categories, brief commentary, and notes for further study are useful supplemental aids. 220 pages.

Simon, Arthur. *Bread for the World.* Rev. ed. Grand Rapids, Mich.: Wm. B. Eerdmans, 1985.

Issues regarding world hunger are presented with solid data, plain talk, and compassion by the executive director of Bread for the World. He gives primary attention to the neglected role of public policy in addressing acute world hunger which, by conservative United Nations estimate in 1974, affects 460 million victims. If people who do not get enough protein or other essential nutrients are included, the number of hungry rises dramatically to between one to two billion people, one-half of whom are young children. This book is for all who ask, What can I do? 179 pages.

Stringfellow, William. *The Politics of Spirituality.* Philadelphia: Westminster Press, 1984.

Stringfellow focuses our attention on what he calls "biblical" spirituality, which entails discerning of and partaking in the activity of the Word of God incarnate. It means being liberated from religiosity of the otherworldly sort and it calls for being deeply implicated in the practical existence of this political world without succumbing to this world or any aspect of this world—no matter how beguiling. Thus, justification and justice walk together. This is a polemical call to conscience and sanity by a noted attorney and Christian activist. His voice and witness live on past his death. 90 pages.

Wallis, Jim. *Call to Conversion: Recovering the Gospel for These Times.* San Francisco: Harper & Row, 1983.

If our discipleship is to be historically relevant, we need nothing short of conversion to a kingdom life-style, declares Jim Wallis, evangelical pastor and founder of *Sojourners.* Evangelicals in this century usually have gone along with the culture on larger economic and political issues. Where the gospel of Jesus Christ is central, our behaviors will be spiritually transformed so that we seek justice for the poor and reclaim our Christian responsibility for making peace.

The key to implementing Wallis's compelling biblical vision is a revitalized Christian community deeply rooted in worship and in the practice of spiritual disciplines. Evangelical theology mixes with progressive politics in an honest, intense, and compelling style. 190 pages.

Wallis, Jim, ed. *Peacemakers: Christian Voices from the New Abolitionist Movement.* San Francisco: Harper & Row, 1983.

The "new abolitionist movement" has brought together an ecumenical group of spokespersons who add their voices to the collective outcry for an end to the nuclear arms race even as their predecessors raged against slavery a century ago. What unites the witness of these 24 people of faith is the urgency of the historical situation coupled with the movement of God's Spirit, which causes them to see their urgent plea for peace to be a faith issue calling for spiritual transformation. 156 pages.

15 Other Resources

Bellah, Robert N., Richard Madsen, William M. Sullivan, Ann Swidler, and Steven M. Tipton. *Habits of the Heart: Individualism and Commitment in American Life.* New York: Harper & Row, 1985.

Four sociologists and one philosopher collaborate in this massive research project, which is widely heralded as a landmark book offering penetrating analysis of the American national character. The malady identified in the American character is an individualism grown cancerous, providing neither joy and satisfaction in life nor grounding for making moral sense of life, as self all but replaces soul. The suggested alternative to this character has to do with a recovery of tradition and meaning, especially as lived out in community through commitment to one another. American spirituality could be a part of that inward turn, but it might also do much to deepen, direct, and discipline that inwardness in the light of faith. 355 pages.

Bilheimer, Robert S. *A Spirituality for the Long Haul: Biblical Risk and Moral Stand.* Philadelphia: Fortress Press, 1984. (Out of print.)

Robert Bilheimer, executive director of the Institute for Ecumenical and Cultural Research, articulates a biblical spirituality in which God always is primary. The direction is not from thoughts, feelings, and experiences reaching "up" to God. Rather, God is made known as a gracious God exhibited both in mystery and clarity. I appreciate especially chapter 15: "The Always-New World of Spirituality in Christ," as well as Part IV: "Spirituality: Being and Doing, United." This is a substantive biblical and theological work. 164 pages.

Cox, Michael. *Handbook of Christian Spirituality: The Major Figures and Teachings from the New Testament to the Twentieth Century.* Rev. and exp. ed. San Francisco: Harper & Row, 1985.
Michael Cox, who specialized in English literature and comparative religion at Cambridge University, offers the general reader a starting point for a deeper acquaintance with the Christian mystical tradition. He rides with the generally accepted definition of mysticism—that is, the direct personal experience of Ultimate Reality, of God. Eighty selected mystics and mystical theologians are addressed. Reference notes, a select bibliography, and index enhance usefulness. 288 pages.

Egan, Harvey D. *Christian Mysticism: The Future of a Tradition.* New York: Pueblo Co., 1984.
Jesuit scholar Harvey Egan reviews the church's rich Christian mystical heritage, focusing on the kataphatic mysticism of St. Ignatius of Loyola, St. Teresa of Avila, and Pierre Teilhard de Chardin, as well as the apophatic tradition as exemplified by the unknown author of the *Cloud of Unknowing*, St. John of the Cross, and Thomas Merton. In chapters 8 and 9 he traces the relationship of Christian mysticism to charismatic phenomena, to psychedelic drug experiences, to the demonic, to perfection, and to contemporary theology. This work is of value not only to academicians interested in mystical theology, but also to persons looking for guidance in prayer and the heritage of mysticism. 438 pages.

Harbaugh, Gary L. *Pastor as Person: Maintaining Personal Integrity in the Choices and Challenges of Ministry.* Minneapolis: Augsburg, 1984.
Claiming that most difficulties pastors face in the parish arise when the pastor forgets that she or he is a person, Dr. Harbaugh

presents a carefully stated and helpfully illustrated vision of pastors as "(w)holistic persons." His model identifies four dimensions of pastors' humanness: the physical, mental, emotional, and social—all integrated in the spiritual. From this wholistic perspective, what may initially be perceived as threat may also be viewed as challenge, calling for choice. The "in Christ" character of pastors' lives with God gives them the courage to take decisive action. Gary Harbaugh is a colleague of mine on the faculty of Trinity Lutheran Seminary, Columbus, Ohio, teaching pastoral care and counseling. 172 pages.

Holmes, Urban T. III. *A History of Christian Spirituality: An Analytical Introduction.* San Francisco: Harper & Row, 1981.

Urban Holmes provides a brief but balanced overview of the wide variety and great richness of the Christian spiritual experience. As previously noted, the amount of writings on the Christian spiritual tradition is large, even if we confine our review to books in English that are still in print. It is easy to become lost in the materials and discouraged in our reading. Holmes does not believe that the legacy of the Christian past is to be reserved only for specialists. There is something there for us all, and we are more likely to make the retrieval if we have a helpful analytical guide who is as concerned to enrich our prayer life as to inform us of our heritage. Before his recent death, Holmes was Dean of the School of Theology at the University of the South. 166 pages.

Holmes, Urban T. III. *Spirituality for Ministry.* San Francisco: Harper & Row, 1982.

In this, his last book before his death in 1981, Terry Holmes—an influential Episcopal thinker, teacher, and theologian—provides both a contemporary theology of the spiritual life and a guidebook on issues such as the disciplined life, living simply, sexuality and holiness, the role of authority, liturgical and personal piety, the relationship to a spiritual friend, and the daily life of prayer. He clearly is concerned with being faithful to a formative tradition while also being conversant with new understandings in psychology, philosophy, and theology. His vision is the spiritual maturation of clergy as integral to parish renewal. In-depth interviews with clergy of representative Christian denominations further strengthens this work. See also Holmes' *Turning to Christ: A Theology of Renewal and Evangelization* (Harper & Row, 1981). 198 pages.

Hordern, William. *Experience and Faith: The Significance of Luther for Understanding Today's Experiential Religion.* Minneapolis: Augsburg, 1983. (Out of print.)
Hordern notes that it is natural and understandable that so many North Americans turn inward to find security and assurance that the outer world cannot provide. But he cautions that no one's experiences are good enough to depend on for security and assurance. Mature faith looks outside the self—to God's good news in Christ—for its assurance. *Experience and Faith* is a clear and powerful message by the widely respected and listened-to president of the Lutheran Theological Seminary of the Evangelical Lutheran Church of Canada in Saskatoon, Saskatchewan. 160 pages.

Johnson, Ben Campbell, *Pastoral Spirituality: A Focus for Ministry.* Philadelphia: Westminster Press, 1988.
Ben Campbell Johnson, professor of evangelism at Columbia Theological Seminary in Decatur, Georgia, examines ministry and all its functions from a spiritual perspective seeking to help pastors (and anyone else interested in pastoral-type ministries) to see themselves anew as individuals called by God, not as those caught in a false professionalism imitating secular counterparts. In the first part of the book he focuses on *being* and the elements that shape ministers' individual personalities; in the second he considers how what they *do* affects their spirituality. In a market where harried and beleaguered pastors often are offered quick-acting magic-like cures for their anemic spirits, this book offers abundant resources and convincing companionship for a gradual rediscovery of spiritual vitality. Seminary students with whom I've shared the work have been positive about it and appreciative for it. 156 pages.

Jones, Cheslyn, Geoffrey Wainright, and Edward Yarnold, ed. *The Study of Spirituality.* New York: Oxford University Press, 1986.
More than 60 writers, representing the Anglican, Roman Catholic, Free Church, and Orthodox traditions, studied the nature and form of individual reverence. Spirituality here is defined as a combination of praying and living as practiced both by ordinary believers

and by those whose special gifts have led to their recognition as saints. Part I on "The Theology of Spirituality" and Part III on "Pastoral Spirituality" frame the larger Part II on "The History of Spirituality." The 634 pages include an index of subjects, index of names, and index of biblical references. This is chiefly valuable as a reference resource.

Leech, Kenneth. *Experiencing God: Theology as Spirituality.* San Francisco: Harper & Row, 1985.

This book is the third in a series, complementing *True Prayer* (1980) and *Soul Friend* (1977). Leech addresses the hunger for an authentic Christian spirituality and invites the reader on a pilgrimage through the Judeo-Christian tradition in search of the God of justice and love. Trained for the priesthood at Oxford, Leech presently serves as race relations field officer for the Board for Social Responsibility of the Church of England. He unfolds a comprehensive picture of spirituality embracing all major pathways. As a pastor he is concerned both with the inner needs of the soul and with the pursuit of Christian discipleship in an unjust world. As a theologian he is concerned to unite theological work with the spiritual quest—the search for a transforming knowledge of God. Leech urges that we develop the facility for turning simultaneously inward to God, who is at the center of our beings, and outward to the children of God, who are made in God's image and are shining in the world. It's an informative and provocative work. 500 pages.

Moltmann, Jürgen. *Experiences of God.* Philadelphia: Fortress Press, 1980. (Out of print.)

One of the most distinguished theologians of our age couples thoughtful reflections on hope and anxiety with two other, more rare, sections from the pen of a professional theologian: a chapter each on "The Theology of Mystical Experience" and "Why Am I a Christian?" The latter, set at the front of the book, offers the author's confession of faith. Dr. Moltmann is professor of systematic theology at the University of Tübingen, Germany. 83 pages.

Moremen, William M. *Developing Spiritually and Professionally: The Pastor's Handbook.* Philadelphia: Westminster Press, 1984.

William Moremen, a United Church of Christ pastor, puzzles with the perplexing question, How can the spiritual and the professional come together? Illustrating the dynamic between these two essentials in the life of ministry, each chapter examines professional concern and spiritual discipline side by side. Chapter titles reveal the coupling: "Reflecting on Career and Discerning the Spiritual Journey," "Studying and Meditating," "Planning and Praying," "Using Time Wisely and Wasting Time Well," and "Attending Meetings and Being Attentive to the Spirit." Moremen suggests we feel those tensions and experience integration before finally letting go of the whole question in the freedom of the Spirit. 119 pages.

Nouwen, Henri J. M. *Reaching Out: The Three Movements of the Spiritual Life.* Garden City, N.Y.: Doubleday and Co., 1986.

According to Nouwen, one of today's most respected spiritual mentors and writers, the three movements of the spiritual life are from loneliness to solitude as we reach out to our innermost self, from hostility to hospitality as we reach out to our fellow human beings, and from illusion to prayer as we reach out to our God. I consider this volume a classic in the literature of spirituality. Its insights are undated, their clarity and depth warranting repeated rereading. Other Nouwen treasures include *With Open Hands* (Ave Maria, 1972), *Out of Solitude* (Ave Maria, 1974), *The Living Reminder* (Harper & Row, 1981; out of print), and *The Wounded Healer* (Doubleday, 1979). 120 pages.

Opsahl, Paul D., ed. *The Holy Spirit in the Life of the Church: From Biblical Times to the Present.* Minneapolis: Augsburg, 1978.

Eight Lutheran theologians provide biblical, historical, and doctrinal perspectives that invite expanding awareness of the Spirit's renewing work in individual lives as well as throughout and beyond the church. Appendixes include documents that speak to developments such as neopentecostalism and the charismatic movement, including statements adopted by Lutheran bodies that cooperated in the former Lutheran Council in the USA. 287 pages.

Palmer, Helen. *The Enneagram: Understanding Yourself and the Others in Your Life.* San Francisco: Harper & Row, 1988.

Helen Palmer, on the psychology faculty of John F. Kennedy University in Orinda, California, provides a definitive but readable guide to this fascinating and revealing method of understanding yourself and those with whom you live and work. Palmer describes the nine personality types in the system, each of which is distinguished by a unique set of mental and emotional preoccupations. Though rooted in centuries-old Middle Eastern traditions, this intricate and dynamic system combines well with western approaches to psychological growth. This work is excellent for opening channels of insight and compassion. 392 pages.

Senn, Frank C., ed. *Protestant Spiritual Traditions*. New York: Paulist Press, 1986.

Seven essayists including Senn, pastor of Christ the Mediator Lutheran Church in Chicago, explore Lutheran, Reformed, Anabaptist, Anglican, Puritan, Pietist, and Wesleyan spiritualities. "Individualism," "superficiality," and "utilitarianism" are often identified as obstacles to the cultivation of a deep spiritual life. Since they also are marks of modern western life, it is not surprising that searches for self-knowledge and self-development, prayer and meditation, and traditions of spirituality should turn to the East and away from those traditions that have been identified with the development of western culture. "In North America the Protestant spiritual traditions especially have been found wanting," says Frank Senn, "because of the dominant role they played in the formation of our way of life." But perhaps the "turning away from" has been based more on presumption than reality. Here are grand heritages that deserve a second look. 273 pages.

Van Kaam, Adrian. *Fundamental Formation* (Formative Spirituality: Volume One). New York: Crossroad, 1983 (not in print). *Human Formation* (Formative Spirituality: Volume Two), 1985. *Fundamental Formation* (Formative Spirituality: Volume Three), 1986 (not in print). *Scientific Formation* (Formative Spirituality: Volume Four), 1987 (not in print).

Adrian Van Kaam, professor at Duquesne University in Pittsburgh and founder of the Institute of Formative Spirituality, has dedicated himself to research, teaching, and writing about formative spirituality for the last 25 years. He defines formative spirituality as "the art and discipline of receiving distinctively human formation and of humanly giving form to life and world." The work is expansive, detailed, scholarly, and for the serious student. Dr. Van Kaam was ordained a Roman Catholic priest in 1947. In 1953 he came to the United States from his native Holland. He is the author of 24 books and more than 100 articles. One has to learn some new language to appreciate Van Kaam, but the effort nets rewards. Vol. I, 330 pages; Vol. II, 271 pages; Vol. III, 406 pages; Vol. IV, 313 pages.

Wakefield, Gordon S., ed. *The Westminster Dictionary of Christian Spirituality*. Philadelphia: Westminster Press, 1983.

From *Abandon* to *Zen* are the entries—terms and descriptions of events, concepts, and persons as well as religious and theological issues in Christian spirituality. More than 150 scholars of international standing cooperate in this comprehensive and authoritative dictionary on the whole range of Christian spirituality, from its roots and first flowering to developments in our own time. The articles, from short paragraphs to multiple pages, are nondogmatic and ecumenical in character. They are scholarly yet available to the average reader. Editor Wakefield is principal of The Queen's College, Birmingham, England. 400 pages.

Williams, Rowan. *Christian Spirituality: A Theological History from the New Testament to Luther and St. John of the Cross*. Atlanta: John Knox Press, 1980.

Originally published in England under the title, *The Wound of Knowledge*, this book emphasizes the cross as the focal point for Christian theology and spirituality. To look to the cross is to look into the darkness in which Christianity has its roots, the darkness of God's being killed by God's creatures, of God's breaking and reshaping all religious language by self-revelation in vulnerability, failure, and contradiction. The work offers probing questions and powerful prose. "Self-dependence is the subtlest mechanism of self-destruction, and to cling to it in the face of grace is a thinly veiled self-hatred." Rowan teaches doctrine and ethics at Wescott House, Cambridge, England. 193 pages.

Notes

Chapter 1: Discovering the Center

1. Joseph Sittler, *Gravity & Grace* (Minneapolis: Augsburg, 1986), p. 25.

2. Quoted by James M. Kittelson in *Luther the Reformer* (Minneapolis: Augsburg, 1986), p. 208. Dr. Kittelson references vol. 37, p. 92 of *Luther's Works*, 55 vols., Jaroslav Pelikan and Helmut T. Lehmann, general editors (St. Louis: Concordia; Philadelphia: Fortress Press, 1955–1986).

3. See second stanza of "Spirit of God, Descend upon My Heart," *Lutheran Book of Worship* (Minneapolis: Augsburg, 1978), hymn #486.

Chapter 2: "Four Types of Spirituality"

1. Adapted from Anthony de Mello, *The Song of the Bird* (Garden City, N.Y.: Doubleday and Co., 1984), p. 96.

2. Most Christians understand that what we have in the New Testament is not one theology. What we get with the four different Gospels, for example, is at least four different theologies—four different ways of looking at that which is beyond words, which defies precise categorization. We are rightly reluctant to exclude any of them. They need to stand in tension with one another. If we accept that there are different theologies that have been part of Christian tradition from the earliest days, why should we not also be open to a variety of spiritualities standing together in tensioned interplay?

3. The Aristotelian philosophy that permeates our Western world's thinking confines knowledge to the five senses and reason. We question any communication that does not fit into these categories. By this philosophy we have limited even our religious experience to the confines of a narrow science of the past. We have lived in a space-time box. But now even the modern sciences of physics and mathematics are no longer limited to the space-time theory. We can surely believe that God is not thus confined. God's ways of speaking are at least as numerous as are our ways of hearing.

4. James Finley, *The Awakening Call* (Notre Dame, Ind.: Ave Maria Press, 1984), p. 123.

5. Anthony de Mello, *One Minute Wisdom* (Garden City, N.Y.: Doubleday and Co., 1985), p. 124.

6. Matthew Fox, "Spirituality for Protestants," *The Christian Century* (August 2–9, 1978), p. 734.

7. Eldon E. Olson, *Spirituality: Christian Varieties from a Lutheran Perspective* (Columbus: Select Publication, 1984).

8. De Mello, *The Song of the Bird*, p. 137.

9. Ibid., p. 101.

10. Ibid., 65.

11. De Mello, *One Minute Wisdom*, p. 138.

12. Ibid., p. 137.

13. Thomas Merton, *Disputed Questions* (New York: Farrar, Straus and Cudahy, 1960), p. 182.

14. Adapted from de Mello, *The Song of the Bird*, p. 130.

15. Reprinted in John W. Doberstein, ed., *Minister's Prayer Book* (Philadelphia: Fortress Press, 1986), p. 410.

16. Adapted from de Mello, *The Song of the Bird*, p. 88.

17. Ibid., p. 163.

18. E. Glenn Hinson, "Puritan Spirituality," *Protestant Spiritual Traditions*, ed. Frank C. Senn (New York: Paulist Press, 1986), p. 165.

19. Quoted in Amand Saintes, *A Critical History of Rationalism in Germany* (London: Simpkin, Marshall, and Co., 1849), p. 51.

20. Frank C. Senn, "Lutheran Spirituality," in *Protestant Spiritual Traditions*, p. 46.

21. Olson, *Spirituality: Christian Varieties from a Lutheran Perspective*, p. 20.

22. Lyle E. Schaller, "The Unraveling of Tradition," *The Lutheran* (January 16, 1985), pp. 4–7.

23. De Mello, *The Song of the Bird*, p. 112.

24. Ibid., pp. 108–09.

25. Adapted from Joseph A. Sittler, *Grace Notes and Other Fragments* (Philadelphia: Fortress Press, 1981).

Chapter 3: Two Views of Spirituality

1. The value of both the vain struggle to free ourselves from the old Adam/Eve life and the equally fruitless efforts to fashion the new Adam/Eve life in Christ is to finally realize that all such efforts are utterly futile. Our personal, dismal failure to produce the Christian life is God's preparation for doing the job God's way.

2. Our hope for victory over sin is not "Christ plus my efforts," but "Christ plus my receiving." Recipiency (openness and readiness to receive God's gifts) is the only worthy posture of the faithful pilgrim. Our part is not production but reception of our life in Christ.

3. In the first three chapter of *Ephesians*, St. Paul asks the saints only to listen while he proclaims that wondrous series of great and eternal *facts* concerning them. Not until he has completed this catalog of spiritual realities about them does he ask them to do anything at all. An evangelical spirituality does not begin with long lists of "conditions" for entering into the blessed life in Christ. Instead, as the primal preparation for leading others into the experience of this life, one shows them what their position, possessions, and privileges in Christ already are.

4. For most of us, it is time to stop asking God for help. God didn't help us to be saved, and God doesn't intend to help us live the Christian life. Christian living is not our living with Christ's help; it is Christ living his life in us. Immaturity considers the Lord Jesus a helper. Maturity knows him to be life itself.

5. Anders Nygren's *Agape and Eros* was the book which opened my eyes and heart to see and appreciate God's unmotivated-by-us love. For some, making this discovery is sudden and dramatic. For others, the realization is nurtured over time.

6. The works-righteousness that Luther attacked was based upon the triumphalist assumption that human beings have sufficient goodness within themselves to earn merit with God. Triumphalism is

always confident of its ability to know and serve God and is certain that God will reward such service. The essence of triumphalism is to believe that God is most clearly evident in the successes, certainties, and victories of life. As Luther saw it, biblical revelation disappoints all of the triumphal human expectations of religion. The Hebrews' faith in Yahweh never depended upon triumphs. Yahweh, they believed, was present in adversity as well as in victory. And in the New Testament, God does not appear in glory and majesty but in a humble, hidden way in the person of Jesus. The cross illustrates the way of God with humanity. A major reason why Jesus was rejected was because he did not come to the world in a triumphal way.

7. Asking Jesus to strengthen us may but heighten our sense of self-control. God does not deliver us from sin by making us stronger and stronger, but by making us weaker and weaker. God sets us free from the dominion of sin, not by strengthening our old Adam but by crucifying him; not by helping him to do anything, but by removing him from the scene of action. Our task is not to beg for help, but thankfully to appropriate that which is already ours in Christ.

Chapter 5. A Spirituality for Our Times

1. The most oppressive demon to be found in the desert, according to Evagrius Ponticus (d. 399), was *acedia*, or "the devil of the noonday sun." It always remains the enemy of the spiritual life, and may again be the most oppressive demon in the desert of our modern life. The term comes from the Greek word *kedia* ("care"), with the alpha privative on front to make it "uncaring." Acedia is boredom, apathy, listlessness, or uncaringness. It is the inability to train and to remain disciplined because we no longer care, we have lost our intentionality, and we give ourselves over to our feelings and our failings.

2. Helen Kromer, "Some Career," from *For Heaven's Sake!* (The North American Ecumenical Youth Assembly, 1961).

Part Two: Our Spiritual Journey

1. Dietrich Bonhoeffer, *Spiritual Care*, trans. Jay C. Rochelle (Philadelphia: Fortress Press, 1985), p. 65.

2. Leroy T. Howe, "Dreams as Spiritual Friends," from *Weavings: A Journal of the Christian Spiritual Life*, II/4 (July–August 1987): 39.

3. Richard Foster, *Celebration of Discipline: The Path to Spiritual Growth* (New York: Harper & Row, 1978), pp. 47, 52–53.

4. William Sloane Coffin Jr., *The Columbus Dispatch*, September 21, 1987, p. 1D.